BRADFORD CITY LIBRARIES

JUNIOR LIBRARIES

Make sure your hands a[...] [...]r
when visiting the librar[...]
Don't make marks in y[...] [...]
Return your book withi[...]
the book again if you ha[...]

This book should be ret[...] [...]ow.

FACTS

AND HOW TO FIND THEM

A GUIDE TO
SOURCES OF INFORMATION

AND TO THE
METHOD OF SYSTEMATIC RESEARCH

BY

WM. A. BAGLEY

SEVENTH EDITION

LONDON
SIR ISAAC PITMAN & SONS LTD.

First published 1937   Fifth edition   1954
Second edition 1938   Revised and reprinted 1956
Third edition   1948   Revised and reprinted 1958
Fourth edition 1950   Sixth edition   1962
                Seventh edition 1964

SIR ISAAC PITMAN & SONS Ltd.
PITMAN HOUSE, PARKER STREET, KINGSWAY, LONDON, W.C.2
THE PITMAN PRESS, BATH
PITMAN HOUSE, BOUVERIE STREET, CARLTON, MELBOURNE
22–25 BECKETT'S BUILDINGS, PRESIDENT STREET, JOHANNESBURG

ASSOCIATED COMPANIES
PITMAN MEDICAL PUBLISHING COMPANY Ltd.
46 CHARLOTTE STREET, LONDON, W.1

PITMAN PUBLISHING CORPORATION
20 EAST 46TH STREET, NEW YORK 17, NEW YORK

SIR ISAAC PITMAN & SONS (CANADA) Ltd.
(INCORPORATING THE COMMERCIAL TEXT BOOK COMPANY)
PITMAN HOUSE, 381–383 CHURCH STREET, TORONTO

MADE IN GREAT BRITAIN AT THE PITMAN PRESS, BATH
F4—(G.27)

PREFACE TO THE SIXTH EDITION

THIS, in an extensively revised edition, with much new and better-arranged material, is a book for journalists, authors, technical writers, teachers, lecturers, students, men and women in Public Affairs, many kinds of radio and television script writers, and all those who deal in FACTS. Admittedly, practical experiment, experience and verbal inquiries must count, but the written word is both the beginning and the end of all forms of knowledge. To preserve our findings, we transmute them to the written, or printed, word. For the same reason, in order to ascertain what others have done before us, to profit by their experience and build on the foundations they have laid, we first consult written records.

Despite the increasing use of visual aids: of the spoken word "on tape"; of electronic "brains," "machine" translating, and the like, the written word still remains the most convenient way of communicating, disseminating and storing information and of referring to it again.

But such are the countless ways in which knowledge is disseminated, diverted into specialized channels and almost submerged by torrents of fresh material the printing presses pour out every day, that one needs training to single out relevant facts from such a maelstrom of knowledge. Journalists, writers, and others in the same category, are professional fact agents. It is their duty to search for, and track down, stray information; to condense it into readable proportions; to interpret its meaning in the light of modern conditions, with reference to a specialized inquiry.

Knowledge is certainly power these days, and for the specialist there is always the problem of keeping abreast of new developments as reported in a torrent of print. And even the specialist has to track down a good deal of general information.

All too often, literary research is associated with crabbed scholars in musty studies or literary eccentrics who pore over ancient parchments on matters of no practical present-day use or who over-read themselves into producing cranky political, religious and other theories. But this touches only one small aspect of the matter. My book is based on the theme that most of the knowledge in this world has, at some time and in some place, been committed to writing. Search out these literary sources and you have the world's knowledge at your disposal; not only on such matters as eleventh-century Burgesses of Bungay or who ate the first banana in Birmingham but

on current scientific, economic, technical and other subjects. The
man who wants to design a better electronic device can, in addition
to working out his own practical experiments, read almost all that
has been written or done about it. Those who first succeeded in
climbing Mount Everest obviously studied all accounts of previous
attempts and profited thereby. No one would say the actual climb
was "book learning": mere armchair study of the *Alpine Journal*.
Yet, without previously published information, the climb would
surely not have been successfully achieved. This point is further
developed in Chapter I.

Even if we are not out-and-out research workers, either professional or amateur, we have often occasion to look up some subject,
especially if we be teachers, lecturers, clergy, or the like. There is a
wealth of material available to work upon but it is very tangled and
we need training to know how to unravel it. In the following pages
an attempt will be made to show the main principles of research.

It is neither possible, nor desirable, to go too minutely into some
of the sources of information as the field is so vast and the approaches
so many, depending on what subject you are interested in. If this
book were being written solely for students of history—to take one
example—and were an annual publication, it would be possible to
give fairly adequate lists of all standard textbooks, reference books,
year books, journals, learned Societies, museums, etc., connected
with the subject as, indeed, happens with the Library Association's
Special Subject Lists. But I presume that only a fraction of my
readers are definitely interested in history. Others may be studying
politics, the life of Robert Burns, magnetism, business efficiency—
anything. A work of encyclopedic proportions would be needed to
provide at all adequate references to every possible subject, and then
it would be out of date the week after the printer received the corrected
proofs of it, so great is the spate of new books.

Certain reference books have attempted the listing of sources of
information by subject in "dictionary" form, but in the main the
contents, though looking "big" and imposing, are not so complete
as they first appear. The most valuable books of this kind are the
ASLIB Directory, the English **Guide to Reference Material** and the
United States **Guide to Reference Books** (all detailed later in this
present book). In all fairness it must be stated at once that these
books do not claim to cover *everything*. What they do set out to
cover (and their coverage is wide) they cover very well. But they are
not reference books to end all further reference work.

It cannot be too strongly pointed out that it is not the purpose of
this present book to provide book lists or reading programmes.

Common sense will show that such lists can only treat general subjects in a general way; well enough for general knowledge purposes but not for detailed and (as often happens) systematic research into unusual subjects. Moreover, such lists can merely duplicate, to a greater or lesser degree, existing bibliographies. It is far better, I think, to give, succinctly, a few well-chosen and typical examples— signposts as it were—than to spread oneself tediously over several hundred pages of a bulky and expensive book. *The reader who follows the instructions and advice given here should be able to trace practically every book that has ever been written on every possible subject, and to find, without undue delay, the right page in the best available book.*

I do not assume that every reader can spend unlimited time on research and is within easy reach of a great library, although professional methods are duly described.

This book gives guidance in research work. It tells of the main sources of information, what libraries to use, how to use the books when they are found. It also deals with note-taking and classification, press cuttings and indexes, and other matters conveniently and concisely. Whilst it treats the subject in such a way as to satisfy the most academic and orthodox, it also contains several practical hints and tips of a kind not usually given in books written by professional librarians.

Previous editions of this book have been favourably received, even by some reviewers, for example, of library journals whom one might naturally expect to be severely critical. Some even recommended the book as a guide for those preparing for professional librarianship, though I should take this opportunity of pointing out that I am not a trained and qualified librarian writing a manual on Reference Library methods, but a working journalist and author: one who must produce, rapidly, factual articles and books on a wide variety of subjects, knowing full well that expertly informed critics await his efforts on every hand. And it is written by one who knows that whilst librarians are almost invariably helpful—often overwhelmingly so—the fact-seeker who is able to find his own way about libraries and other reference sources can get his facts more quickly (and time is money) than one who is tied, so to speak, to a professional librarian's apron strings.

Most books on specialized aspects of "information" work are—as they should be—written by professional librarians. This layman's book treats the matter from the "receiving end." The present writer is therefore well able to identify himself with his readers and understand their needs and problems.

It must not, for one minute, be thought that this book is intended to show how the research worker can teach the professional librarian his own business. Were it not for skilled librarians (and their professional associations) we would not have the fine reference "tools" so generally available today, nor even the library facilities we take for granted. Let me here pay tribute to those librarians whose enthusiasm often goes beyond their paid duties. By getting to know how to use reference books expertly you can help the librarian to help you better. He wants the books used. As an informed reader you will use the books more.

In the present volume, the books mentioned are given as examples only. Further examples can be seen from bibliographies in the manner to be described.

Generally, only so-called "standard books" have been cited, and—while discrimination has been exercised—those mentioned should be regarded as typical only. New books, however, appear almost daily; older books are revised periodically. Therefore, readers desiring the latest information should specify the latest edition of the work I mention, or one similar to it. Since all works quoted as examples are of a "steady" nature, this book is not quickly out-dated.

It is, however, a good practice always to ascertain whether a supplement has been published to any reference work. Bear in mind, too that though some reference works grow old they are often kept up to date by means of a card index or the like, in some large libraries. Further, some long-established books, e.g. **A Dictionary of Anonymous Literature** are often still rightly remembered by the name(s) of their original author(s) (in this case Halkett and Laing) although new editions made many years later have different editors.

Such journals as *The Times Literary Supplement*, *The Guardian Weekly* and *John O'London's* regularly review or notice books of library-research interest. Not all standard reference books are reviewed in the lay press, however, and they are sometimes formally noticed only in specialized Trade and Professional journals. When such reference books are reviewed in the National newspapers it is usually because they contain some special article or preface of controversial and newsworthy interest. Some readers may recall the great consternation caused by the publication in **Burke's Peerage** of an article which hinted that, theoretically, it was possible for H.R.H. the Duke of Edinburgh to receive the title of King. The fearless prefaces to **Crockford's** commenting on the current relations between Church and State, usually ensure that this work receives publicity.

On the whole I have kept to English books and sources though I have included a certain number of U.S.A. reference books which are fairly well known and usually available in English libraries.

Since it is presumed that the vast majority of readers of this book will be using public libraries, I have not hesitated to mention some standard books which are now out of print. In any case, such books, if required for the home library, can usually be obtained after a little search, from the better-class antiquarian booksellers.

Most of the books I mention are standard text and reference works. Occasionally, however, I have mentioned an obscure or limited edition book to show what *has* been done in the way of specialized bibliography, etc.

It is particularly gratifying to be able to launch this book on yet another edition: not from reasons of personal pride or gain, but in the knowledge that the work, forged in the fires of my own hard-won experience, has proved itself of continuing use and value to literary research workers. There is nothing in it that I have not personally practised, professionally, for many years, with profit.

The revision, for this edition is a major one, almost a new book, in fact, with a completely new chapter on sources for technical writers and the rest of the book brought as up to date as possible; for the techniques of fact-finding do not stand still. Since this book was first published there has been, for example, a remarkable development in library co-operation (duly noted as with other developments in these pages). ASLIB then hardly more than a mere fledgeling has gained great strength and increasing status. More and more industrial firms have established research libraries (though there is still much slack to take up). One has only to glance at the *Situations Vacant* columns of certain periodicals to see how much technical writers—members of a comparatively new profession—are in demand.

Abstracts and Digests of scientific and technological subjects have certainly proliferated. When this book was first written, not many people thought much of Russian achievements in science. Now the shelves of science libraries are sagging under the weight of well-produced Science Abstracts (in English) from Iron Curtain countries.*

There has been a welcome increase in the use of microfilm techniques and other methods (dry copying and the like) for bringing copies of rare material in one library to a research worker far distant.

* The National Lending Library for Science (*see* p. 71) possessed, when opened, more books in Russian than in English and the emergence of Chinese publications is expected to be a major factor in science literature in the next hundred years.

I have already alluded to such things as information "on tape." Electronic aid has now come to the assistance of the translator.

The anonymous and unacknowledged "ghost writer" who once wrote (and very often invented) most of the autobiographies of celebrities has often, nowadays, the status of a named co-author (". . . as told to . . ."). Others are given the title of Research Assistant.

In the past, a kindly soul tentatively put forth a scheme whereby some kinds of patient and plodding research could be done on a free-lance basis by retired business and professional folk. This may still apply. In fact, I hope it does. But nowadays we get young and alert private organizations providing technical and commercial abstracting and information services not already covered by other organizations.

Most public libraries find that the issue of non-fiction books is well maintained and the circulation of more serious-minded (that is, more fact-filled) periodicals and newspapers tends, if well managed, to rise when that of sensation-mongering and muck-raking ones tends to drop.

Before me, current as I write, is an *Observer* article reviewing British book production for the past year. One notes that ". . . the emphasis in publishing is moving steadily towards the factual and the useful; people and institutions want information for themselves and for instructing others . . .. Technical handbooks were nearly three times as numerous as in the 1930's."

Similarly, under a heading: "*Facts are the Best-Sellers,*" the *Daily Telegraph* reports from the U.S.A. that non-fiction books published there run almost twice as high as fiction among "best-sellers."

Nor is the trend confined to the intellectuals. *Punch*, in an article "Top People's Reading" (18:1:61) reports that the best-selling weekly and monthly periodicals are currently those which supply the demand for FACTS.

For many years past, advertising Agencies have analysed data from various questionnaires or obtained by persistent young ladies who quiz housewives at their front-doors. Many large Agencies now employ a worker whose first concern is to glean all *published* information about the market prospects of a certain commodity.

Despite what the Jonahs may say, modern youth is better educated than it was, and this means better informed tutors and better technical libraries and so on. All such trends (and I have listed only a few of the more obvious) mean more work, amateur or professional, for those engaged in fact-finding. This necessarily implies more efficient fact-finding.

Further, by making himself a real authority (albeit often an anonymous one) a research worker can often find scope in contributing to reference books.

For an explanation of the arrangement of this work, *see* Chapter XXI.

It is perhaps too much to hope, in such a vulnerable technical book as this, that all oversights have been detected. I have, in the past, been grateful to those readers who have given constructive criticism and I have usually been able to incorporate their suggestions when a further edition of this book was called for. I hope that this happy state of author-reader co-operation will continue.

It is confidently hoped that the present revision will not only win for itself new readers, but will also merit the renewed attention of those who have already found previous editions useful.

PREFACE TO THE SEVENTH EDITION

ADVANTAGE has been taken in this edition of the opportunity to bring this book once more up to date by the addition of information on further sources which have become available to the seeker after facts.

CONTENTS

CONTENTS

CHAPTER I

THE WORLD OF KNOWLEDGE

"Now what I want is, Facts. Teach these boys and girls nothing but facts. . . . Stick to facts, sir!"

Thus spoke Thomas Gradgrind, "a man of facts," in Dickens's *Hard Times.*

We need not pursue Facts with the same grim determination as Mr. Gradgrind, but there is little doubt that the affairs of the world today are based upon facts: the assimilation of old facts, and the finding of new. Although in these restless days, when old ideas crash overnight and new ones come in breathless succession, we might wish that things would slow down a little, we must realize that in order to keep mankind's energies and mental powers tuned up to concert pitch, opportunities must be found for exercising them.

New ideas; new facts; new methods. The well-oiled machine in constant use lasts far longer, and is a far better thing than one allowed to suffer the rust of disuse. Although there are thousands of new facts, most of them are combinations and permutations of old ones. An army of research workers is at work tracking down these facts, rescuing them from oblivion, classifying them and offering them anew to the world.

Most of the knowledge of the world is enshrined in books or other written and printed matter. The wealth of this material is amazing, and one of the first things that a student of research work must realize is that the information sought is usually printed somewhere. The task, of course, is to find *where.*

People write books for many reasons. Authorship is an honourable profession, and books are often written for the money they will bring. Other writers make writing their hobby; they are often able to undertake the writing of books which could not have been written as a commercial proposition. They are truly "labours of love." Professional people, such as school teachers, judges, artists, stage folk, etc., like to epitomize their experiences and knowledge in a book. It serves to add to their professional status and set a seal upon their skill or talent. Professional societies publish valuable "papers" containing information of great value and help to their members. Government departments publish reports of national interest. Newspapers and periodicals peddle information for its general interest. The facts contained therein may be of considerable importance, affecting one's livelihood or mode of life or thinking. Very often the facts are just retailed for our distraction and diversion.

To supply all these books and papers, research workers are getting the facts. Here again, they may be of several kinds, amateur and professional. The most obvious example is the journalist; not so much the one who specializes in flighty articles such as "Do Women Make the Best Wives?" but the one who writes technical and "fact" articles. Journalists can be said to be the middlemen of the "fact" industry. They seek out the facts, sort them out, and pass them on at a profit. The journalist who writes an article on "The Tea Trade of Ceylon" is often quite unconnected with any commercial enterprise, and if he made the revelation that three-quarters of the plantations were in the last stages of bankruptcy, he, personally, would not be in the least worried or concerned. His readers might be, particularly if the article were in a trade paper.

Again, although in actual practice the writer usually has some good knowledge of the matter before he writes the article, this is not always the case. The writer, sensing that such an article was topical, and a profitable "market" awaited his writings, might set out to get the information, although his present knowledge of Ceylon and the tea trade was very elementary. In order to work on a business basis, he can afford to spend only so much time on research. Yet he succeeds in writing an authoritative article on the matter. How is this?

People who think they are "in the know" say, "He gets it all from books and other people's magazine articles and newspaper cuttings." The first implication is that he steals another's ideas. It is as well to answer that charge straight away. The tracking down of items of information is a skilled task. He has to pick out the relevant items from a great mass of material. This demands training and skill. Furthermore he ropes in isolated but related items, and views them in a new perspective. He invests the material with his own personality, or, in the case of more staid and impersonal publications, with the authority of whatever society or body he is working for. The research worker must avoid becoming a mere hack.

The second implication is that it is delightfully simple to copy extracts from others' books. This is generally absurd, for one must know what books to look in, where the books are to be found, how to find them in the library, how to find out what part of the book to read, and how to absorb the information thus located. Put this "knowing one" in a fairly large library and ask him or her to track some simple fact, such as, for example, when did Chopin compose his "Funeral March"? The result is usually pathetic. The would-be researcher is utterly lost in a forest of books. He or she might make a wild plunge into the contents of the nearest bookcases, or thumb over the catalogue in a hopeless manner. Behold the surprise when the trained research worker goes almost instinctively to the right book, and the right page in the book.

Many large industrial and commercial enterprises have their research departments where business and technical books and magazines are stored. The information thus culled is available for planning new projects and developments. Another field involving much research is in the cinema studios. On the one hand we have laboratory research (a sphere which does not at the moment concern us), whilst on the other hand, seeing that the studios have to create an artificial world of their own, involving all countries, times, and peoples, information is always needed as to what these people wore, looked like, etc., so as to secure the right effect. What kind of headgear did Turks wear in 1780? What does a Chinese laundry in San Francisco look like? Did women wear riding breeches in 1840? What kind of forks did the people of Queen Anne's time use? What does a silversmith's shop in Shanghai look like? All these questions the studio research worker will answer.

Then there are social surveys, which are held not merely to amuse the surveyors, find employment for the funds of various trusts, and satisfy a queer enjoyment of statistical computation and tabulation, but rather to satisfy a scientific desire to know certain facts in an accurate and orderly way so that they can be applied to the better understanding of social and economic conditions and organization. Facts which do not, in some way, increase useful knowledge are not much good.

This is particularly so in the case of scientific and industrial research. It is all very well for a scientist (possibly in a Government-sponsored research station) to investigate—shall we say—some problems of street-lighting. It is all very impressive when, in smart typographical dress, a Report is issued, and all very efficient when the Report is filed, down to the last dot of decimal classification, in some library and finds its way into bibliographies and abstracting-service publications. It is all very enterprising for a technical journalist or science writer to retrieve this published knowledge, and gratifying if interested people read it. But unless the knowledge is acted on, and it leads as in this case, to better street-lighting, it is not much use. Of course, some proposals, all right in theory or on small-scale laboratory tests, are not acceptable as large-scale industrial propositions. The prevailing trade or intellectual "climate" may be against the acceptance of some new ideas and, in fact, many "new" developments in, say, medicine have been triggered off, or sustained, by reference to previous almost-forgotten, reports. Some ideas, whilst not acceptable in themselves, can act as stepping-stones towards newer ideas. But, in general, it can hardly be denied that too little use is being made of the vast amount of knowledge that is recorded hourly. There are, as just hinted, various reasons for this and, in turn, there are several remedies. Since this present book is neither one on industrial practice nor technical writing, the only thing the research worker as such, can do, is to so gather his facts that others will be encouraged to promote them.

There are many people who engage upon research purely as a hobby. They do not intend to sell their information. They do not intend publishing it for their own glorification and for the propagation of their ideals. They just find interest in following the paths of knowledge. Exercising the mental powers is just as important as physical "keep fit."

They are not usually "bored stiff," like many shallow-brained folk are today when deprived of artificial amusements such as the cinema and organized games. This present volume is not intended to be one in praise of book-reading: rather is it a treatise on reading for hard facts as opposed to beauty of literary style (unless, of course, your inquiry is concerned with literary gems), although, whatever one's interests, one can find inspiration, diversion, and pleasure in the glorious company of books.

The curiosity of children is well known, and some of their posers parents find difficult to answer. Curiosity and observation invoke pleas of what-why-where-when-how-who? all day long. This is a healthy sign of a growing mind. Usually, when one becomes older, one falls into a rut, and has few interests outside one's trade or profession. Indeed, in many of these, the notions and ideas are very limited and effete. They are sheltered under the name of "trade secrets" sometimes. A few of these mysterious "secrets" (which any research worker could soon discover) hide the lack of real modern information and ideas.

Sometimes when we see "Letters to the Editor" about such abstruse subjects as Hindu mythology and Peruvian sun-worship from Lt.-Col.'s and other unlikely people, we are apt to smile and regard them as mild cranks. What is the use of all this out-of-the-way knowledge? You may as well ask what is the use of knocking a little white ball round a field with a club? One is physical exercise, the other is mental exercise. They both give pleasure. With the growing knowledge of various founts of information we can attain speed and confidence in research. On the one hand we shall not be too disappointed if the search proves harder than we anticipated.

On the other hand, we shall not plod hopelessly on when the information desired is too obscure to be worth while, and the time better spent otherwise.

Especially when trying to deal with "official" sources (e.g. some aspects of the last World War or some aspects of recent Foreign Policy) we may well find that those who might be able to help seem, to us, to take an unduly "stone wall" attitude to our inquiries. There may, be some real reason for this negative attitude. There may be obscure reasons for not releasing any information not obviously a top military or diplomatic secret. The research worker who is on top of his job, however, often finds that where one source of information is closed, another (less obvious) may be open. He may often find that the initial rebuff from officials is just a "hedge" against the possibility of public servants being officially involved with irresponsible sensation-mongers. If he can prove he is a *bona fide* research worker he is sometimes given (albeit guardedly) official information that was originally refused.

At the beginning of this chapter it was stated that the research worker should be aware what a vast field of book material there is for examination. Another point to realize is that there is far more spirit of helpfulness and goodwill, especially in the world of learning, than is generally thought. Partly this is due to a sort of free-masonry among intellectual workers, but if we are sceptical enough to analyse these "good turns" we shall find that there are other causes.

Individuals may give you information because they are flattered to think that you regard them as experts. Business concerns give it to you because it creates goodwill, which is an advertisement for them. Public officials often take a broad view of their duties. The officials of public libraries are paid to help you, but apart from the fact that they are paid to do it, they are mostly enthusiasts over their job, and are only too glad to be of assistance. As a rule they are organized for a better service of information than is at present demanded. Make friends with the librarian in your local public library. He knows more about his stock of books than you will ever do, and he can prove a useful ally.

The point behind the old joke: ("Do you keep carpet tacks?" "No . . . we sell 'em!") has present-day application to libraries. The old-time librarian *kept* books for use of the privileged few. The modern librarian, if one will excuse the use though in a complimentary way of a current colloquialism, is out to "sell" (or) share out the culture to be found in books to as many as possible. Although the following passage (taken, with acknowledgement, from the bulletin of Edmonton Public Libraries and Information Services (note the latter part of this title)) . . . may seem a trifle high-flown it is, as each phrase is studied, perfectly true. "Opportunity and encouragement is here freely available: to continue our lifelong education; to keep abreast of progress in all fields of knowledge; to maintain freedom of expression, and a constructively critical attitude towards all public issues; to be better social and political citizens of our own country and the world; to be more efficient in our day-to-day activities; to develop our creative capacities and powers of appreciation in arts and letters; to aid generally in the advancement of knowledge; and to use our leisure time to promote personal happiness and social well-being."

The librarian does not care what you want to know, or why. He assumes that you have real need of the information. Few people enter a reference library to ask irrelevant questions. Tell the librarian your requirements *exactly* and then he will get you the most suitable books from his stock. If you are vague, you will waste his (and your) time, by causing him to get the wrong books.

If, for example, you are doing research work on the love life of leprechauns, *say* so. If you merely murmur something about leprechauns you will cause the librarian to get a pile of books about folklore in general, and that of Ould Oireland in particular, possibly to no purpose. Your inquiry may well involve a specialized aspect of folklore or possibly some aspect of philosophy or mythology. The librarian gets such a lot of routine questions (e.g. what is the population of Wolverhampton?) that he is usually glad to use his expertise in an unusual one.

Books, and other sources of information, are like tools. We have to learn not only what tools to use for a certain job, but the right way to care for them, hold them, and manipulate them.

Tools, whilst having great potential uses, are of little value if kept permanently boxed up in a warehouse or hopelessly jumbled. In the same way, facts stored in libraries and the like, should be methodically and efficiently gathered and then translated into *action*. There are some self-styled "practical" men who profess a disdain for all "book-knowledge," holding that anything put in a book is henceforth dead and entombed. We need not devote much time to discussing the fallacy of this contention since what, one presumes, these people really object to is that so many people cram themselves with learning and then make scant practical use of it. Provided one keeps a sense of proportion, there can be no real objection to accumulating "escapist" knowledge for one's own private satisfaction, and this present book would certainly help such a reader. But it is chiefly concerned with the practical world of today. It shows you how to get your facts, and expects you to *use* them.

The well-informed man is not so much the marvel who has a phenomenal memory, as one who knows exactly *where* to get the required information. What we ought to know is Knowledge. What we can find out is Information.

CHAPTER II

THE USE OF LIBRARIES

IT is presumed that the reader is already a book-lover and uses the local public library. If not, steps must be taken to rectify this immediately. Browse round the shelves, particularly those in the less-used parts of the library. Find out how the books are shelved and catalogued. Find out whether there is a reserve stock of more rare or lesser-used books. Particularly use the Reference Room. Note well what directories, year books, annuals, etc., are taken. You might even strike up an acquaintance with the librarian. Let him know you are a research worker. Do not be afraid to ask for more than the usual number of books (provided you really need them). If the books are not in the library, ask for them. They can usually be obtained on loan for you, especially if your library is in the National Central Library network.

Get to know what different publishers issue, especially those who specialize in the books in which you are interested. Read the book reviews in the better-class Sunday newspapers; in *John O'London's*, in *The Times Literary Supplement* and so on and notice any books that are likely to interest you. Get to know books!

Membership of such an association as The National Book League may prove useful. At various places in this present book, bibliographies, etc., issued by the N.B.L. are mentioned.

As the aim of this present book is "meaty" *conciseness*, I have not here the space in which to describe the lighter and "human" aspect of what, in a formal book-list (possibly with necessarily curt annotations) may seem rather ponderous reference works. The "inside story" of the founding and development of various encyclopedias and reference books and personal stories of the original Roget, Chambers, Whitaker, and the like (I anticipate, of course, in naming them at this stage) are not only interesting but help endear the books to us. We feel as though we were asking advice from a wise old friend. Such stories have been written up from time to time in various places, but since past volumes of *Punch* are fairly easily available, I content myself with referring readers to certain such articles (lightly written but not in any way "comic"), taken at random—

Light in Dark Places (on John Timbs), p. 117, 23rd July, 1958.

Try Under "Diabolical" (on Palmer's Index to *The Times*), p. 131, 9th Sept., 1959.

Verify Your References (various standard reference book), p. 36, 7th Nov., 1960.*

The introductory essays which precede bibliographical lists in such compilations (all referred to in the present book) as the National Book League's **Reader's Guides**, the Penguin **Reader's Guide** and the U.S.A. **Good Reading** are worth studying. We find our way about much more easily in the field of, say, Biography, if we understand something of the aims, purposes and methods of the most successful biographers, and differentiate between *biography* and *personalia*.

Visit Libraries

Visit all the libraries you can. Note their specialities, methods of shelving and cataloguing. You will soon begin to feel at home in a library. A great number of people still think that public libraries work on the "one ticket—one book" system. The privilege of borrowing books to take home is reserved for ratepayers as a rule, but usually anyone can use the Reference Department, and research workers are always made welcome. Books from the Lending Department are sent up to the Reference Department if required. Note whether there is a "Reader's Advisor" in addition to a Reference Department staff. Try to find out their respective functions.

We may find that the libraries of many societies and institutions, not nominally open to the public, and even the entirely private collections of book-lovers are often available to the genuine research worker if the material is not available elsewhere. A courteous request is seldom snubbed, though membership of ASLIB (*see* Chapter XI) is a particularly useful "passport" to many specialized libraries.

Certain reference books, catalogues, bibliographies, indexes and the like, are kept in the Head Librarian's office, or behind the Inquiry desk. Though chiefly for the use of those compiling library catalogues and so on, they are usually available for readers.

On your first visits of exploration to a Reference Department (presumably of a Public Library) you can either just browse around (the Librarian in charge will be quite used to people doing this and will not "bother" you), or you can try a bit of easy research work either on some topic you know well . . . your work or your hobby or else on something that you would like to know more about: possibly some topic broached on the radio or T.V. If in the course of looking up something about, say, tropical fish, you find yourself looking into a book on Mexican Folk Art or one on Small

---

* *See also* (same source) **Another Good Year for Year Books** p. 55 9th Jan., 63. Also **How Much Can A Capitalist Lift?** (*Mulhall's Dictionary of Statistics*), p. 167 30th Jan., 63.

Arms Manufacture . . . so much the better (at this stage). Reference works on Photography, Italian Proverbs, Circus Arts, Estate Agency, Swedish Dentists, Prisons, Cookery—look at them all. The best way to learn about books is to handle them.

There are several general books about public libraries, such as W. J. Murison. **The Public Library.**

Another useful small book giving a general survey of library history, and method is—Leyland, E., **The Public Library: Its History, Organization, and Functions.**

Your local public librarian will be only too pleased to recommend others. A number of works (noted in previous editions of this present book) have been written about great libraries, but these tend to date. Up-to-date information is available in librarian's journals. For example, in the year or so previous to the re-issue of this present book, the *Library World* published articles on such great libraries as those of the British Museum, the Bodleian, the National Library of Wales, the National Central Library, the National Institute for Medical Research, the Ministry of Education, the Patent Office and the London Library, giving details of their collections, method of cataloguing, their staff, and so on: information of interest to the "lay" research reader as well as the fellow-librarian. Your local public librarian will let you see copies of this journal and, of course, other journals of this kind containing similar information.

As befits a capital city, London is well provided with libraries of all kinds, and it may well be that the present writer, cossetted with such facilities, has taken too sanguine a view of library facilities elsewhere. It is quite possible that the majority of readers of this book do not live near a great and famous library. But few are out of reach of the public library, even though it be represented by a once-weekly mobile County Library.

Inter-Library Co-operation

Few users of public libraries are aware of the co-operation now existing between most libraries. Quite apart from the fantastic cost involved, no *one* normal public library could possibly take in, catalogue and house *every* new book and *every* issue of a thousand or more periodicals. Each co-operating library, therefore, agrees to buy all (or as many as possible) books on subjects allocated to them. One library, for example, takes in—and in all languages, though this cannot be said of some other libraries working, perhaps, on a slender budget—all books on Population, International Law, and History and Travel of Middle Europe. This, of course, is in addition to books it buys on all subjects for its own general stock, and is also in addition to any special collections it may have. [*See* further, Chapter XV—with regard to co-operation on periodicals.]

The combined stocks of about 600 urban, county, University and special libraries in England and Wales can—as briefly alluded to a page or two back—be drawn on through the agency of the National Central Library. There are similar schemes operating in Scotland and in Northern Ireland.

Thus, no matter where you live, you can, provided you are prepared to wait a week or two and, perhaps, pay postages (in whole or in part), obtain practically any book you need if only you make full use of public library resources. If necessary, the National Central Library will try to obtain a book from a co-operating library abroad.

Most public librarians welcome suggestions for new books and on many occasions, books that I have asked for, and which were not in stock, were specially purchased.

Further to another previous brief reference, it is well worth remembering that the Reference Department of a public library can be used freely by any caller, regardless of his residential status. If, therefore, you find (as did the present writer) one Reference Department (now, I am glad to say, being rebuilt) housed in a frowzy room with old-fashioned book shelves holding far too much ageing stock (though still containing useful information), you can go to another, only (in a large town) a mile or two away perhaps, where remarkably up-to-date stock is kept in attractive surroundings, and equipped with writing desks and the like.

Your small-town library *may* be a dingy relic of the Mechanics' Institute Reading Room of yesteryear but, very often, a not-too-long journey to the nearest large town will bring you into contact with a really well-equipped library where such *reference* works as encyclopedias (not usually available for home-lending) can be consulted. After all, some research workers give up the whole, or part, of their annual holiday to work in libraries abroad.

Provincial research workers coming to London—perhaps for the day only—to glean information from the larger libraries would be well advised to inquire, in advance, the hours of opening and whether a special ticket is required. At the Patent Office Library there is no formality other than the signing of a book, but at the British Museum Reading Room, special application supported by sponsors must be made for a Reader's Ticket. Permission to use the Reading Room for a day is usually granted to a *bona-fide* research worker provided that the applicant can prove that the library facilities he requires are not available elsewhere, at a smaller library. It is unwise to presume on this concession however.

The libraries of Universities are primarily for the use of residents, but they are often open to other students. As we have seen, however, the studious layman can, if necessary, have access to University libraries through the N.C.L.

The British Museum Reading Room

The first thought of anyone having any research work to do, and living in and around London, is to apply directly to the Reading Room of the British Museum. Except during the early morning, and late in the afternoon (when it is too late to order any books), the great circular room has normally its complement of about 500 readers. As already stated, so great is the congestion that to avoid impedance of genuine literary work by casual readers, the Museum allots tickets only to those who can show that they have definite literary work in view, and that they cannot do it elsewhere. No genuine research worker need fear that he or she will be frozen out of the Reading Room. Rather should this restriction be welcomed in the interests of research workers. In many ways the Museum Library is unique, but in some ways the same, or even better, service is offered by smaller, specialized libraries. The present writer uses quite half a dozen libraries besides the British Museum Reading Room. Because he, a Londoner, refers continually to *London* libraries, it must not be assumed that he is unaware of, and has not used, the fine provincial libraries.

One thing that invariably vexes the newcomer to research work in the larger libraries is the time taken to get the books. One should bear in mind that many of the lesser-used books are stored some minutes' walk away, and have to be located. (Indeed, in such a library as that of the Patent Office, the older periodicals are stored in a separate building and a few days' notice has to be given by those wanting to see them.) In a large library several hundred readers may be wanting several hundred books and staff is limited. This is another reason for trying the small libraries first. Although the book requisition form may be dispatched by pneumatic tube, the books have to come on a trolley pushed slowly by hand. It is a good plan to devote one visit to looking up the catalogue numbers of the books one may require, and filling in the forms for future use. In most libraries books may be ordered in advance, and, after a day's use, reserved again. Alternatively, one can take some other work to get on with whilst waiting—some proof corrections, writing, etc.—since many libraries have spacious desks. A few even have study cubicles.

Librarians usually try to arrange their books so that those most in demand are nearest to hand. Thus in the British Museum Reading

Room, there are thousands of standard works on the ground floor, to which readers have open access. Books next likely to be in demand are on the upper gallery shelves, and so on.

Private and Subscription Libraries

The real advantage of a Great library is that one is likely to find all the books one requires—and especially rare and out-of-the-way books—in one building. It is, as I show, quite possible to do all normal literary research work through public libraries (and a great deal through one's own personal library), though either through snob reasons or (let us say more charitably) from ignorance of what facilities public libraries now offer, some people prefer the private subscription libraries, especially in the matter of fiction. These, of course, can be useful in addition to the public library.

Inter-library loans do not necessarily apply to current fiction, and although a public library may order several copies of a novel or popular memoir, there may be a waiting list (with you near the bottom!). This present book has scant concern with those who wish merely to cut a fashionable figure by being the first to read the "latest," but it is sometimes essential, for professional reasons, to be in the van of modern fiction.

The subscription libraries run by various large stores are well known. It will often be found that some libraries of this type offer a class of membership (naturally at a higher rate) in which any recently published book not in stock will, within limits, be obtained on request. Get particulars and compare the relative advantages.

The century-old London Library with its half-a-million books over a vast range of subjects is a noteworthy institution catering for literary research. Subscribers can keep out as many as twenty books at a time.

Lewis's Medical, Scientific and Technical Lending Library, also over a century old, is well known and, like the London Library, issues a catalogue valuable not only to actual users of these libraries but to bibliographers in general.

Libraries in London

An extremely interesting and useful book even for those who do not live or work in the Metropolis is the Library Association's **The Libraries of London** (ed: R. Irwin and R. Staveley). The extended treatment given in this work will help to amplify many matters only, of necessity, briefly mentioned in this present FACTS . . .

CHAPTER III

A PRELIMINARY SURVEY

THE things in this world are very closely interwoven. Science is not confined to the experimenter's laboratory, but is allied to Industry. Industry suggests Geography—the sources of raw materials, location of factories and works, the places where the goods are to be sent, etc. History is allied to Biography. So we could go on, but the point to be established is that, in research work, we must analyse each inquiry, for it may contain two or more composite facts requiring reference to two separate sources.

Take, for example, a simple inquiry: Who was the reigning monarch of England when the "Rocket" made its maiden journey? We have to find out when the "Rocket" was run, and this may be done by looking up some book on transport or railway history, or else looking up the inventor, and then referring to his biography. Having ascertained the date, it is a simple matter to complete the second part of our question.

Some inquiries are, of course, much more complicated than this.

Analysing an Inquiry

For example, supposing you were engaged in compiling materials for a satirical or comic history of Snobs and are doing the job fairly thoroughly. (Such a book, has, I think, been written fairly recently, but we will assume that existing works are, in your estimation, inadequate.) As most people with a smattering of literary education know, Thackeray wrote a classic **Book of Snobs,** so one obvious source is Literature. But even if we found other snobs in the works of, say, Dickens, we should, for a well-balanced book, include some representative snobs from Modern Fiction. There are all kinds of snobs . . . the musical, the golfing, the "old school tie" and so on. This may mean reference to works on Music, Sport, Education, and the like. The study of snobbery is, I suppose, a kind of *Social Survey*, and, very often, the best people to "see ourselves as others see us" are witty foreigners who write books on *Life and Customs of the English*. This may well involve *Translations*. Does snobbery depend on Economics? Does the practice fluctuate with different periods of History?

14

What have others said on Snobbery? Can you find it in such a work as the **Britannica Syntopicon**? (*see* Chapter XII) or in a book of *Quotations*. Will your *Press-cuttings* file help you? Snobs can be (unknown to themselves), quite funny. Can books on Humour help you? Many a true word is, as we are so often told, spoken in jest. Will any *After-Dinner Stories* or *Jokes* be illuminating?

Surely such a satirical journal as **Punch** will prove a rich field for snob-research? What about other *Periodicals*? Did the **Reader's Digest** ever tackle the subject?

Have *snobs* been the subject of an *Essay* old or new, British or foreign?

What are your *Personal Experiences* of snobs? Can you add something *new* to the research? What, incidentally, IS snobbery? Is it always a bad thing? This is a matter of Philosophy. What is—finally—your *Personal Opinion and Summing-Up*?

The above thoughts are jotted down completely at random and by no means do more than just skim the surface for those wishing to delve deeply.

The research worker should therefore bear in mind that whilst bibliographies and other published aids are extremely useful (the whole purpose of my book is to commend them!) they will not automatically solve all problems. Except for the most humdrum extraction of basic facts from standard reference books, much research depends on the worker having a lively and inquiring mind . . . the ability to see every aspect of the subject. Greater skill comes with the appreciation of the many (but not always obvious) sources of information available, and the knowledge of how to use them. Whether your approach is academic or "popular" depends entirely on your personality, and, of course, the purpose for which the information is needed.

Note, in the foregoing example (on Snobs) the expression "for those who wish to delve deeply." In view of what is to follow, it should be pointed out that whilst it usually pays, especially when dealing with an "obvious" subject, to ferret out some *unusual* information (and so give some freshness to the matter), practical considerations usually limit the extent of the research and the time that can be spent on it. Especially in one's novitiate, one can "spread" oneself luxuriously over a very wide field of published information, as by this means one gets to know various sources of reference. But when one is on the actual "job," keep strictly to the point. Does the inquiry merit five minutes or five months (or, with some profound specialists, five *years*)?

Work from Simple to Complex

This is another golden rule. It is all very well to find out, as will be described later, that an article on a subject you are interested in appears in an obscure century-old country newspaper, the files of which can be seen in a library many long miles away. A book in your own library is much better. If not in your own library, then in the local public library, and if not there, in one of our larger libraries.

Similarly, save yourself as much trouble as possible by working from simple to complex in the actual selection of books. If you have pared down your query to essentials, as indicated at the beginning of the chapter, you should have a clear idea of what you are looking for. Look up the matter in an encyclopedia or appropriate Year Book first. Often your query is solved right away.

Suppose you are looking for a description of a town so small that it warrants only the briefest mention in an encyclopedia or gazetteer. Upon further search, you find a popular tourist handbook to the county in which the place is situated, and also a ponderous tome "The History of the Manor of——" written in the middle of last century, describing the place in tedious detail. You will naturally look in the simple guide book first, but if your query remains unanswered, look in the larger book.

Suppose the query still remained unanswered. The "tome" probably mentions sources from which the information derived, and you will then track down these to see if the information you want is among them. You might want to know who first built the now-ruined priory, and your search takes you among old deeds and parchments. You may then get what you want. But suppose you spend hours among the musty documents only to find that the information is given in the encyclopedia, the county guide, or some standard work such as the *Victoria County History*, a fact you could ascertain inside a quarter of an hour!

Look, first therefore, in the most likely place. Work from the broad to the narrow.

Our general line of inquiry is this—

1. What *exactly* am I looking for?
2. What books, etc., will help me?
3. Where can I get these books?
4. How shall I find their position in the library I choose?
5. How shall I extract the maximum information with the minimum trouble?
6. How shall I record and store this information?

There are other questions such as—

7. How shall I sort out and rewrite this information?
8. How shall I dispose of it? (Book, lecture, lesson, etc.)

but it is obviously not within the scope of this work to deal with the actual writing of books and articles. It is our aim to gather the straw before we can make the bricks.

9. Assuming I cannot find any mention of my subject in printed books, where else shall I inquire (personal inquiries, etc.)?
10. Where can I get illustrations, portraits, etc.?

In the following pages, an attempt will be made to show how these questions can be answered.

CHAPTER IV

LIBRARY CATALOGUES

THERE are many systems of classifying books and papers, so that the research worker will, until experience is gained, usually spend a good deal of time in locating the books or their press numbers. The time is not really wasted, since it all helps to gain experience in library work. Should one become hopelessly fogged, the help of a librarian or assistant should be sought.

Books may be classified under—

1. Author.
2. Subject.
3. Author and Subject combined in one alphabetical series (perhaps with Titles, too). This is called "Dictionary" cataloguing.

The notes which follow show some general principles.

Author

Anonymous authors, or those who write under initials, etc., are nuisances, and a thorn in the side of an otherwise perfect form of catalogue, and the one most used. Assuming one knows the name of the author, one merely finds the name in the catalogue and runs down the list of works until the desired one is found.

If we do not know the initials, we shall be lucky in having an author with a not too common name. If his name is Smith, Brown, Dubois, Müller, etc., we are in for a long search among many hundreds of entries. In this case, it is quicker to look in the subject index. For example, suppose we are looking for a book (title not known) which has something to do with monotype machines by a man named Wright (initials not known). The quickest plan is to look in subject index under Printing or Typography, and see if there are any books by a man named Wright. Bibliographers who give references to authors, without their initials, such as SMITH, "An Introduction to the Study of Heat," are not very helpful to the layman although, when a book has become "standard," the librarian usually regards the author's initials as superfluous and refers to him by his surname only.

Foreign celebrities are indexed under the English form of their names, e.g. VIRGILIO, Joannes de. Such French names as Guy de Maupassant are likewise arranged as MAUPASSANT, Guy de, but with British personal names, the appendage is retained, e.g. De

Courcy (which occupies a place between Decourcelle and Decourde-marche), and MacDougall (even if the author writes his name as McDougall). R. S. S. BADEN-POWELL is entered as POWELL, R. S. S. BADEN. The author of a book "by W. A. B." would be entered as "by B., W. A."

Noblemen are often cross indexed under both their family name and their title e.g. DISRAELI and (Lord) BEACONSFIELD. St. is usually spelt out as *Saint* and Dr. as *Doctor*.

Very often the papers of a society, etc., written by an individual, but on behalf of the society, have no author mentioned. The society is the author. A little experience is needed to track down some of these anonymous works. They are often grouped under various headings: catalogues, encyclopedias, directories, liturgies, hymnals, etc. Almanacs are listed as "Ephemerides." Publications of International Congresses are under "Congresses." An anonymous work entitled, say, "The Book of the Caravan," might be listed under "Caravan" in an author catalogue.

Laws and Official Documents are usually entered under the names of the places they concern, with a sub-heading of the issuing authority.

See also in this present book, notes on *Alternative References in Index* and on *Newspapers* and *Periodicals* in the British Museum. If you can manage to see a copy, the **Simplified Cataloguing Rules,** a mimeographed publication issued (my copy is dated 1959) by the Private Libraries Association, is useful and instructive.

Anonymous and Pseudonymous Books

To trace these, the following are useful: Halkett and Laing, **Dictionary of Anonymous and Pseudonymous English Literature,** (this useful reference book is now published in a new edition with various supplements which brings the whole work up to 1956, and now includes modern books from the U.S.A.). Stonehill, **Anonyma and Pseudonyma.** Marble, **Pen-names and Personalities.**

Subject List

To many research workers this list is more important than an author list. We have often to gather some information on a certain subject. We do not know, or care, *who* wrote the books, provided they are good ones. A subject list is indispensable in this case.

How are the books to be grouped? There are many thousands of headings we could classify books under. A small library having, say, six books dealing with tools, could group them with other books dealing with general engineering and handicrafts. A large technical library might have a hundred or more books on the subject. There might be books on Ancient Egyptian Tools, Machine Tools used in Stone Cutting, modern Carpenter's Tools, Hints on Grinding Tools, etc. Each, apparently, is a group in itself.

Decimal Classification

Of all the systems tried out at the large libraries, the most widely used method of classifying books is the Dewey, or Decimal, system (or some form of it). In this, all books are classified under one of the following heads (it is usual to class fiction and sometimes to class biography separately).

000	General Works.
100	Philosophy, Psychology.
200	Religion.
300	Sociology, Law.
400	Philology.
500	Natural Science.
600	Applied Science.
700	Fine Arts.
800	Literature.
900	History, Geography, Biography.

Now by subdividing these main classifications (by adding a second figure) we can further classify a book. Engineering, for instance, is a useful art (600), and is indicated by 620. Agriculture is another useful art, 630. Medicine is 610. There are several kinds of engineering—civil, marine, hydraulic, etc.—so a further subdivision of 620 is called for. Thus mechanical engineering is 621. Machine tools, as a branch of mechanical engineering, calls for the subdivision 621·9.

One could go on subdividing almost indefinitely. For example, the classification for the packing of photographic filters is 771·356·004·3. Where two subjects are in alliance, the two codings are joined by a:, e.g. the reference for a work on the "addition of *chloroamines* to *ketenes*" would be 546·171:547·387. The / sign is used when, for example, 774/776 covers the sequence 774, 775 and 776.[1]

In many libraries only the first three or four letters of the classification are actually marked on the spine of a book, though the full classification is usually written on the inside book plate. The classifying of complicated subjects is, of course, a matter for those trained librarians who specialize in cataloguing. By noting the Decimal Classification of one's special subject, however, one is able, especially in highly scientific studies, to pin-point, at once, references in various Abstracts (*see* Chapter XI). Bear in mind, however, that whilst, say,

---

[1] Slight differences may occur between British and American practice.

references to the technology of whale by-products will come under one classification, the subject of International Law regarding whaling may well come under another, and the history of old-time whalers come under yet another.

At first acquaintance some of the classifications may seem odd. For example a book on the "Tramways of Croydon" and a Postage Stamp Catalogue are both classified under Social Sciences. A little reflection will show why these classifications are so.

The handbook necessary for the operation of the Dewey system is somewhat expensive but an abridged (and cheaper) version (actually of the U.D.C.) is published by the British Standards Institution and is very convenient for the private user for classifying his own library. There is also a later, modified, version.

Whatever critics may have against it, the advantage of the Universal Decimal System is that it is *universal* (for all libraries, etc,) subscribing to it. To have to translate a foreign work may be an unavoidable legacy of Babel. But to have to "translate" classification numbers, especially in technological subjects, is just stupid. The reason why some great national libraries still retain their own numbering systems is probably because these were well established long before Melville Dewey propounded his scheme in the 1870's and the task of re-numbering literally millions of volumes is rather too formidable.

Form of Catalogue

For all usual purposes, a card *index* is best, on account of the ease with which the cards can be withdrawn, altered, added to, etc. These cards should be handled by the *edges*, not the tops. This preserves the cards from tearing and finger marks and enables them to be turned over more easily. Some filing cabinets have a sheet of glass or perspex suspended just above the contents to compel users to use the sides of the cards.

Many of the cards you now see in the index are supplied, already printed, by the British National Bibliography Ltd. Others, relating to Government publications come from H.M.S.O.

Make quite sure you are using the right catalogue. To avoid congestion some filing cabinets in the Lending Department of a public library may contain index cards relating only to books acquired during, say, the past ten years, or for books actually shelved. For older books (possibly in store) there may be a separate catalogue.

Books Withheld

It can be taken for granted that in all good libraries the catalogues reach a high standard of accuracy, but there are occasions when one suspects the catalogue to be wrong or not brought up to date. It is not often one can fault a catalogue, however. Certain books might be purposely withheld. It may not for example be the policy of a great research library to issue modern fiction until it is so many years old.

In the British Museum Reading Room, entries for modern fiction appear in the Catalogue as soon as any other current entries, although there are restrictions on its issue to readers.

Some private diaries and papers are left to libraries on the condition that they are not available to the public until (say) fifty years after the author's decease. This is obviously a safeguard against offending (or even libelling) any living persons. But whether for example, an M.P. in the exercise of his public duties and not as an author, could gain access to such normally withheld information, is a moot point.

Some books may be obscene or in some way unfit even for this broad-minded age. Those who wanted to borrow them would have to show special reason.

See Alec Craig, **The Banned Books of England.**

Library Difficulties

One cannot learn the lay-out of a library and its method of cataloguing in one brief visit. As a rule the librarians are extremely helpful, but now and again the inexperience of a subordinate assistant causes friction, and should this happen, one should inform the superintendent. To avoid looking for a book or paper in some inconvenient place, assistants have been known to affirm that the book desired is "in use" or "on loan." It is difficult to prove that it is not. I should hasten to add, however, that most juniors in a library (if they have found their true vocation) are only too willing to be of some service. It makes a welcome "break" in some of the inevitably humdrum things a junior must do.

CHAPTER V

BIBLIOGRAPHIES

"WHAT books are there on the subject?" This is one of the first things a research worker asks. For preparing "study outlines" such lists are also useful if well arranged. Bibliography is, strictly speaking, the *science* of books, which includes the study of typography, book-binding, illustration, paper, etc., although it is now generally applied to *lists* of books. But for such bibliographies, libraries would be in a chaotic condition, and our research work made very difficult. Since books are published every week, it is impossible for any printed list to be absolutely up to date, and there are many occasions where it is necessary to refer to the latest book on the subject. It is quite easy in such an event, to look up lists of "books in print" (*see* next chapter).

Bibliographies in many subjects must, to a greater or lesser extent, list a number of old books since books on, say, the history of Peru are not published every week. In order to compile a representative selection of them, one must range backwards.

The average research worker generally requires a not-too-long list of books of fairly recent date covering his chosen subject, and books that are ready to hand. If his local library is an "open-access" one, he can go at once to the shelves where all the books on one subject are grouped together (usually by U.D.C. classification), bearing in mind, of course, that in a lending department some of the books (possibly those that will be most useful) may be out on loan, and also that "oversize" books may be on a special deep shelf. He can check by looking up the subject index of the catalogue. The choice of books of course, is limited by the stock held by the library.

It therefore follows that a library subject catalogue is, in effect, a series of bibliographies or, at least, book lists. It can be presumed, in most cases, that the books were carefully selected before being added to stock and old ones are weeded out, and so, for example, a list of (say) the seven books on angling in the local branch public library constitutes a simple bibliography of the plain Book-List type on that subject.

Many public librarians compile, with regard to books actually in stock, bibliographies on local history, celebrities, and industries: on subjects in the news and so on. My local public library has just issued a bibliography on Model Railways—a hobby, I presume, currently popular. The Dagenham (Essex) Public Libraries have issued a special catalogue on Music and Musicians—a subject of special interest to the Librarian here and to his colleagues. The Gillingham (Kent) Public Libraries have issued a bibliography on Marriage and Homemaking, which goes beyond being a mere book list and is quite a "social document." These bibliographies (which other Libraries can consult) are good—if random—examples.

A London Bibliography of the Social Sciences is a subject catalogue of a group of nine London libraries and compiled at the London School of Economics. It is the largest subject bibliography of its kind.

The larger the library the greater number of books it can draw on for inclusion into bibliographies. The subject index of our greatest national library—the British Museum Reading Room—can therefore be regarded as the nearest approach to a truly comprehensive National bibliography. Here the number of books, old and new, English and foreign, on Angling and its cognate subjects (to continue with our original example) must run into several hundreds . . . if not thousands (I have not counted them).

If we had such a subject index-catalogue of a large library we would not expect to find more than a tiny fraction of the books therein listed actually in a local library, but it would enable us to ascertain what books *have* been written on the subject and, if our inquiry were a specialized one, to see whether certain of the books listed could be obtained by, say, an inter-library loan.

For this reason, the catalogues of the libraries of such Public and Professional bodies as the London County Council, the London School of Economics and, of course, the British Museum, are used by other libraries. It is hardly likely that the library of the Royal Institute of British Architects would be lacking in any of the best books in its field. It can be safely assumed that it has a highly specialized collection with much unique material.

Whilst Tulsa, Oklahoma, is a long way from London, England, its local library's *Petroleum Bibliography* is to be found in some of the larger science libraries in Great Britain. [For Science bibliographies, *see* Chapter XI.]

The "Recent Additions" lists of the big libraries are well worth studying. In addition to carrying *book* lists, some contain a précis of, or otherwise call attention to, noteworthy articles in specialist journals.

In passing, it might be remarked that one can purchase, from Washington ready-printed catalogue cards of books in the Library of Congress, (which contains books deposited under the U.S. copyright law and also certain worth-while works from other countries).

As most of the cards include a list of chapter-headings or some other indication of a book's contents, they often form useful bibliographies.

They can be supplied retrospectively and one can, in ordering the cards, specify a subject or an author, as, for example, "All 20th-century books on Astronomy" or "All books by Zane Grey." One cannot, however, ask selectively for "the best books on astronomy" or "the titles of the most famous and best-selling Western stories."

Bibliography v. Book List

Lists of books in subject catalogues are not true bibliographies, however. In the first place a bibliography is usually selective, though this is a variable term. A group of German scholars once prepared a *select* (not exhaustive) bibliography of Shakespearean studies which contained more than four thousand items. Fortunately for the average research worker, not all bibliographies are so extensive.

Secondly, a good bibliography usually takes a wide view of its subject. A bibliography of, say, Chaucer would probably contain not only a list of works actually by that writer, but such things as anthologies, children's versions, commentaries, criticisms and translations into other languages. There might be lists of dictionaries of archaic words and of characters; a gazetteer of places, and the like, to be found in the author's work . . . and so on. It would also, if an extensive one, cover such "background" matters as everyday life in Chaucer's England and note some contemporary writers. It would possibly include the publications of any Society devoted to the study of the writer's work.

Such writing around the subject is usually suffixed with *iana*, e.g. Chauceriana, and on, presumably, the principle that the English language has *le mot juste* for everything, a bibliography containing, additionally, critical notes, is often termed a *Catalogue Raisonné*.

See R. L. W. Collison **Bibliographies: Subject and National.**

Annotations

A good bibliography should, I think, be well annotated, especially where the title (and subtitle) give little or no clue to the book's contents. The title and subtitles of the book you are now reading gives, if I may say so, a clear indication of the book's contents, but such a title as "A Land" even if included in a bibliography on Physical Sciences would mean nothing without such an annotation as "An interpretation of man's relationship with nature as revealed in the geological evolution of Great Britain" (quoted from **Good Reading**). Unfortunately annotation even in scholarly lists, is often done perfunctorily, as for example—"A useful book by a renowned authority." Would a worth-while list include a useless book by a discredited hack-writer? Admittedly it is not always easy to sum up a book in about thirty words (the often-recommended limit). An annotation, by the way is not the same as an abstract (*see p.* 64).

Readers' Guides

Before we go too far ahead, we might deal, here, with a matter that is rather important to the student. Whilst a good bibliography on, say, "The Modern Irish Theatre" will cover the subject very well, a student may object: "What I really want is a short list of hand-picked standard books for intensive study. Were I at University, my tutor would give me a Reading List. Will the bibliography therefore act the part of the tutor in suggesting 'required' reading?" In other words we need a Reader's Guide.

Students of such well-defined subjects as Archaeology, Philosophy and Sociology, etc., are, as regards "basic" books, fairly well catered for. From the dawn of "popular" Culture in Victorian times and onwards, many complications of the "Courses of Study," "The Hundred Best Books" type have come and gone. Penguin Books have now published **The Reader's Guide,** wherein a panel of well-qualified scholars and experts in their fields, advise how (in introductory surveys) and what (in over 1,800 descriptive recommendations) to read in eighteen fields of knowledge and interest. The lists are not confined to volumes published by Penguin Books.

This follows, very closely, the U.S.A. publication **Good Reading,** normally obtainable in England as a paperback (Mentor Books). It is sponsored by the Committee on College Reading. It contains over thirty sections of book lists, each prefaced by an educationist. Though many of the books are issued exclusively by U.S. publishers, there are sufficient available in English editions to make this paperback book useful.

Athough a good teacher should always be on the look-out for new books on his subject, most tutors prefer, for coaching in basic studies, a text-book that "wears" well. It is this type of book that mainly appears in such bibliographies as **The Reader's Guide** and **Good Reading.**

Many (especially technical) books contain useful bibliographies as an appendix, or as footnotes. These lists refer to books which, in turn, have their own bibliographies appended.

Where requisition slips have to be filled in (giving name, date, author, and press-mark of book), as at the British Museum Reading Room, it is wise to file and keep them.

The advertisements on the back of the dust jacket of a book dealing with, say, an outline of Spanish Art, may also refer to others on, say, French or Italian Art.

Prospectuses of various examining bodies (e.g. the City and Guilds of London Institute) often contain useful lists of books recommended for students' reading.

A note on the uses of old bibliographies soon follows, but we may anticipate it and mention here, for convenience, the following books.

A useful and classified list of selected books on all subjects is Sonnenschein, W. S., **The Best Books**, Six Parts, London, 1910–35.

An out-of-date, but at times still useful, book is **Standard Books**, 4 vols., 1912–13. Edited by Tweney, C. F. An annotated and classified guide to the best books in all departments of literature, with a copious index of subjects and biographical notes of authors. (T. Nelson & Sons.)

Another of this nature is Forbes Gray, W., **Books That Count**, 2nd Edition, 1923. A dictionary of standard books.

The Best Books for the Year—established in 1914 and, discontinued through the ensuing War, started again in 1929.

Bibliographies in Antiquarian Booksellers' Catalogues

The annotated catalogues of the better-class antiquarian booksellers often reveal interesting bibliographies as this extract from a list of Howes Bookshop (Hastings) shows (I have omitted the prices, as these are irrelevant to the present purpose).

CHEMISTRY.—Ferguson, John.—**Bibliotheca Chemica:** a catalogue of the Alchemical, Chemical and Pharmaceutical Books in the Collection of the late James Young.

The knowledge accumulated by Ferguson in forty years of reading in the works of early chemists was poured fourth in these volumes.

CORNWALL.—Boase, G. C. and Courtney, W. P.—**Bibliotheca Cornubiensis.** A Catalogue of the Writings, both manuscript and printed, of Cornishmen, and of Works relating to the County of Cornwall.

Bibliographies of English Literature

As an example of *subject* bibliography and also, of a famous reference book, readily available, we may cite—

Bateson, F. N. W., [Ed.] **The Cambridge Bibliography of English Literature** (familiarly referred to as the C.B.E.L.).

This, under the sub-headings of Drama, Fiction, Poetry, etc., gives in chronological order (e.g. the Nineteenth Century), lists of the most important books written about them. Under each author's name are listed bibliographies dealing with his work.

A Concise C.B.E.L. (Ed. George Watson) is also published—a bibliography of the more important works of English literature from Caedmon to Dylan Thomas in a single handy volume which contains the essence of the full (five volume) work.

There is also the **Annual Bibliography of the English Language and Literature** edited for Modern Humanities Research Association (Cambridge University Press).

Subjects Covered by Bibliographies

The compilation of book lists or of more elaborate bibliographies is, as one may naturally imagine, a favourite occupation of many librarians. Some of the bibliographies are published in full book form. Some are in the form of varityped sheets well bound up. Others are just cyclostyled clipped-together sheets. The latter might well be just as valuable as the more expensively-produced efforts.

Practically all the most popular subjects (and not a few outlandish ones) are covered by excellent bibliographies and there are few persons of note, ancient or modern, who have not been "covered" by one or more bibliographies.

The bibliographies (published in full book form) held by any individual public library are more or less confined to chance acquisitions. In one library I have just visited, there are bibliographies of Dancing, Food, Heat, Circus and Allied Arts on a shelf in the reference Library. Many more, however, might be filed, if they consisted of cyclostyled sheets. Make your requirements known to the librarian.

Finding Bibliographies

The first problem to be solved, therefore, is—Has a bibliography been compiled or can it be compiled to order for the subject you are interested in? The second problem is—If such a bibliography exists, where may it be seen?

Bibliographies of Bibliographies

So many bibliographies have been written that it has become necessary to compile a catalogue of them, i.e. a bibliography of bibliographies. All libraries have, naturally, a list of bibliographies they possess but it is often necessary to go farther afield.

See Besterman, Theodore, **A World Bibliography of Bibliographies.** 3rd and final edition 1957. As the title indicates, this is subdivided by languages and authors. This is a masterpiece of documentation and is again referred to elsewhere in this present book. It covers bibliographical, catalogues, calendars, abstracts, digests, indexes and the like.

Useful because it is cumulative and issued frequently is the **Bibliographic Index,** a **Bibliography of Bibliographies,** a U.S.A. production from the H. W. Wilson Co.

When it comes to Reading Lists "made to order" members of the National Book League and (for scientific and technological subjects), members of ASLIB have obvious advantages.

The National Book League issues several Readers' Guides (i.e. an essay by a well-known authority, followed by an annotated book list) on such subjects as Modern China, Space Exploration and Crime Detection. It also issues multigraphed annotated book lists on such subjects as Education, Sea Shells and Monastic Orders. For its members, the N.B.L. will (if the inquirer cannot be referred to existing bibliographies) compile book lists of (usually) recent English books on particular subjects.

Occasionally (though this source cannot always be tapped) a newspaper specialist writer (e.g. on Financial Affairs) may be able to give a short list of good, recent books (possibly those he, himself has recently read) on, say, Unit Trusts.

Union Catalogue of Bibliographies

Fortunately, owing to inter-library co-operation, we have such a work as the **Union List of Reference Books and Bibliographies** (Ed. Payne, L. M. and Harries, J. M.) a selection of 800 bibliographies, etc., with locations in Metropolitan and Greater London Libraries.

With this (or something similar) as a basis, aided by supplementary information which it is the librarian's professional business to record, it should not be too difficult to trace the location of any desired bibliography. If the desired work is in a library too far off to visit personally, and if the work cannot be sent to you on loan, it is often possible to have photo-copies made of the relevant pages.

Old Bibliographies

As already hinted, no bibliography can include the very latest books for with the passing of every year, new books make their appearance. It is an axiom among most Reference librarians, however, that no bibliography is ever too old to be of *some* service and may be invaluable in tracing long out-of-print books. But if the latest available bibliography on a certain subject was published in 1920 (and you have made sure that no Supplement exists, albeit in MSS., somewhere) you are at least saved the trouble of checking books published *before* 1920. With the passing of the years, publishers' catalogues (*see* next chapter) become more and more inconvenient of access.

As a very rough working rule, most Reference librarians in general non-specialist libraries keep, ready to hand, Book Indexes covering at least the last five years (and possibly up to ten years). Many inquirers, especially at the more specialized libraries wish to go much farther back than that: in fact, some want to go back before the date of the first Whitaker's catalogue. A biographer or editor of, say a definitive, complete edition of the works of Alexander Pope may wish to trace little-known poems that have somehow escaped the notice of others or to exclude wrongly-attributed items. It is then that old bibliographies (some of which I will now note) come into their own again.

Other works which might be consulted as occasion requires are Watt, R., **Bibliotheca Britannica,** four volumes, Edinburgh 1824, Peddie, R. A., **Subject Index to Books Published up to and including 1880** (Third Series, 1939). Thus, if we wish to look up books on, say, Trigonometry, we turn, dictionary-fashion, to this heading—it is preceded by *Trier, Trieste, Trifels,* and *Trigonometers*—and find listed, first a book by Lansberg (1631); then one by Cavalieri (1638); then one by Oertel (1690), and so on, the last entry (second series volume) being a book on trigonometry by Redt, published in 1880.

Peddie's **Subject Index,** though out-dated so far as *recent* books are concerned, is of perennial service in looking up *early* books on a number of subjects. The whole three series should be consulted, the entries being different and complementary to one another.

See also Courtney, W. P., **A Register of National Bibliography,** three vols. (London, 1905–12). This contains a useful list of references, including periodical publications, arranged alphabetically and chronologically by subjects and topics. It is a large, laborious work, and, in spite of its title, is international in outlook. Vol. 3 is a supplementary work.

CHAPTER VI

BOOKS IN PRINT

PREVIOUS editions* of this book to which those interested are referred,† contained details of catalogues enabling us to trace many, if not all, books from the late fifteenth century to the time (comparatively recently) when books were systematically recorded. It is felt that, in the present edition, the same space can more usefully be employed in giving more details of present-day book lists, since these will be more useful to the average reader.

Book Lists

Several very useful compilations are now available, at first glance somewhat duplicating and rivalling each other, but acquaintance with them shows that each has its own useful characteristics. One may appeal to the bookseller who is concerned only with checking the title and author of a book and finding out whether it is currently *in print*. One may appeal by announcing new books quicker, though another may be more scholarly. One may announce more books, but another may be more selective. One list may appeal more to a research worker who wants to know whether such and such a book has been published at all (presumably it will then be in some library).

The Bookseller trade journal, published by Whitaker, includes, in its last weekly edition of each month, a **Publications of the Month,** containing books newly published or old books reissued, being given alphabetically under both author and title (i.e. a book on *Bells* may be followed by a book written by someone named *Belmont*). Then follows an abbreviation indicating a broad classification of the book, e.g. Fic(tion), Rel(igion), Eng(ineering). We can thus follow here new books weekly and monthly, as well as in another (monthly) publication, **Current Literature,** from the same publishers, which reviews new books and records books classified in numerous broad categories, (e.g. Art, Politics, Religion, etc.) by *Author*. The information in the above two journals is then collated in **Whitaker's Cumulative Book List** (started in 1924). This appears quarterly and lists all books published Jan.–March, Jan.–June and Jan.–Sept. Then comes the annual volume, a complete record and classification for the year of

* e.g. the 3rd.
† See **Government Publications** catalogue for new British Museum "Short Title" issues.

all books (excluding some minor cheap booklets and specialized Government and other papers) published in this country. The annual volumes are still further cumulated.

The Reference Catalogue (also from Whitaker) is affectionately known in the trade as the "booksellers' bible." In its present form (adapted in 1936) it is a large index volume recording full bibliographical details of all books *in print*.

The British National Bibliography (from 1950) is of great value. Its objects (to quote from its Preface) are to list every new work published in Great Britain; to describe each work in detail and to give the subject-matter of each work as precisely as possible. The work is carried out at the British Museum by a team of fully-qualified bibliographers. Cumulations of the weekly edition are published every three, six, nine and twelve months and is thereafter cumulated (e.g. 1950–54).

Classification is on the Dewey Decimal System. Its publishers (The Council of the British National Bibliography, Ltd.) represent the British Museum, The Library Association, The Publishers' Association, The Booksellers' Association, The National Book League, The British Council, The Royal Society, ASLIB, The National Library and the U.N.E.S.C.O. Co-operating Body for Libraries.

The listing does not include cheap trash. Neither does it include periodicals, maps, or (generally) Government publications.

There are in any case, adequate reference books to all of the above. For example, reference to *Paperbacks* catalogues is made in Chapter XX of this present book.

The English Catalogue of Books sponsored by the Publishers' Circular, Ltd., is a *continuation* of the London and British Catalogues and records in one alphabet under author, subject, and title, the size, price, date of publication, and publisher of books published in the United Kingdom from 1801 to date.

It is now published quarterly and cumulates half-yearly, yearly and four-yearly.

There has been no suspension during the past century and a half, although the Second World War caused some delay in publication.

It is a valuable and much-used work of reference. Some volumes list, also, the publications of Learned and other Societies. Later volumes list maps and atlases.

An important U.S.A. reference book, published in New York, is **The Cumulative Book Index.** This is a list of books in the English language published anywhere in the world and consists of an author, title and subject catalogue in one alphabet. It appears in monthly and (cumulatively) half-yearly, yearly and four-yearly forms, though frequency may vary. It includes selected pamphlets and Government publications.

Publishers' Catalogues

Most publishers specialize. Some specialize in technical books, others in business books, books on building, religion, topography, fine arts, etc., and, besides dealing in their own books, act as agents for the leading U.S.A. and foreign publishers of books of a similar type. Their catalogues (obtainable gratis on application) are usually well-produced and classified, often with a summary of the contents of each book, and, although the range is limited by the books that the publishers have in stock and in print, they nevertheless contain lists of great value. The advertisements in the backs of some books are worth looking over too.

The catalogues of the better-class second-hand booksellers are worth getting (*see* Chapter XX).

Foreign Literature

French, German, Italian, etc., book lists are normally available in this country. Books in most European languages are published in Britain, both for the foreigners with us and for export. Details of many of these appear in the British trade lists; others sponsored by the British Council and H.M. Stationery Office, from whom details of these latter can be obtained.

Brinkman's **Cumulative Catalogues** (in Dutch) are well known in the great libraries. The big booksellers who do appreciable business in foreign books usually have foreign booksellers' catalogues available.

CHAPTER VII

ENCYCLOPEDIAS AND DICTIONARIES

ENCYCLOPEDIAS form some of the more obvious sources of information, but not everyone uses them to the best advantage.

Types of Encyclopedias

Before embarking on a course of study on any particular subject, one would do well to read up the matter first in a good encyclopedia, where a broad and "meaty" survey is given, often by renowned experts.

Bibliographies are often given for further reference, whilst there are usually many cross-references to other articles in the book. When one is studying a fairly broad subject such as Art, or Electricity, dozens of cross-references will be required, and *the index must be used*. Because articles are arranged alphabetically many people think that an index is not needed. In fact many would be surprised to know that an encyclopedia *has* an index. They might think it a joke like the old chestnut about the savant who wrote an index to the dictionary.

Encyclopedias have not always been divided up alphabetically. The actual word means something like "complete education," and in ancient times, encyclopedias were intended to be read right through. As time went on, and knowledge increased, and also as learning became more specialized, reading (and mastering) an encyclopedia was a very tall order. So, for easy reference, the matter was split up alphabetically.

This system cuts both ways. The advantage is that if we know a good deal about electricity but only want to refresh our minds about dynamo construction, we look up *Dynamo* right away, and there is the matter, clean cut. On the other hand, if we know little about electricity and wish to know about dynamos, the matter referred to under this heading will naturally not be fully understood. We may not know about electricity and magnetism, inductance, direct current, alternating current, etc. These will have to be hunted up, and it is best to look first under the general heading of *Electricity*, both in the encyclopedia and also in the index, and then see what other articles we are to be referred to to complete our survey of electrical matters.

The Children's Encyclopedia is a work which is not alphabetical. Electricity is treated as a whole. By referring to the index we can ascertain where *Dynamos* are mentioned.

Most encyclopedias give information under the name of the smallest subject, not under the largest theme, but there are important exceptions.

Out-of-date Encyclopedias

Most books are strictly speaking, out of date before they are published. This particularly applies to books dealing with current affairs. Biographies, etc., are not so affected, but it is inevitable that between the time the writer hands the proofs to the printer and the time when the book is in circulation—a matter of some months—fresh events have occurred. A book may have a short life. If it has a reasonably good sale, neither the writer nor the publishers care. It is easy to revise or rewrite it.

Not so an encyclopedia. For one thing, it is costly, and one looks upon it as an investment. New encyclopedias are issued from time to time, but the private buyer does not usually like buying a new one every few years. With public libraries it is different.

Old encyclopedias are useful in ascertaining the state of knowledge at the time of issue.

Some research workers prefer older editions of the **Britannica** for certain subjects, e.g. the ninth and eleventh editions for expert articles with historical accounts.

When new matter is added to an encyclopedia in the course of revision, something must go, as the pagination of the volume must not be disturbed. Some articles are therefore condensed and others deleted. Biographies of lesser lights often suffer. If you cannot see what you want in a modern encyclopedia, it *may* be in an older one.

As a general rule, the research worker dealing with modern subjects should consult the very latest editions at a public library.

Some publishers' claims to "revision" should be approached with caution by the serious student. Are *all* the entries revised? Will one revised article be cross-referenced to a non-revised one?

Many great libraries do not encourage mere *reference* work (such as can be undertaken in the excellent reference rooms of local public libraries), but rather *research* work. Encyclopedias are provided on the open-access shelves, but for the very latest editions one has to apply for the volumes in the usual way. It is not expected that readers will use the open-access encyclopedias for prolonged study. It is unfair to other users. Extra copies are often available if application is made.

There are many kinds of encyclopedias, some general, others dealing with specialized matters only.

General Encyclopedias

The most famous is probably **The Encyclopædia Britannica,** despite (in the view of some critics) its now American "slant." It is kept up to date by annual Year Books. (Speaking generally, editorial staffs of good encyclopedias stress "background" or "basic" facts and avoid those which will rapidly "date." The place for constantly changing data is in frequently-published directories, year books and the like). A book by Herman Kogan on **The Story of the E.B.** has been published.

Chambers, and **Everyman's** among the English, and **Americana,** the famous multi-volume **Italiana,** the German **Brockhaus** and **Meyer** and the French **Larousse** among the foreign, are much esteemed.

There are many others, English and foreign. The more "popular" they are, the more likely they are to contain mistakes. Even the best books have a few errors, and the research worker is likely to perpetuate them if facts are not checked from other sources.

One should look up several different encyclopedias, as the treatment varies greatly (according to the editors' estimate of the importance of the items, and the space available), and all the essential facts of the matter are not necessarily embodied in one particular work. Many scholars hold one famous encyclopedia to be quite incomplete in some respects.

There are some who maintain that encyclopedia articles should not be too long, since then they usurp the functions of more specialized works and (as just hinted) run the risk of "dating" quickly. The present writer would not like to be too dogmatic about this, as the scrappy information in some small encyclopedias can, on occasion prove irritating. It is not a bad idea to look up, in as many encyclopedias as you can, some subject in which you are already fairly knowledgeable and compare.

Checking References

A few hours before writing this, I had occasion to look up *Piano-Accordion* in various encyclopedias. Almost everyone knows what this still popular musical instrument looks like. It is a development of an earlier instrument now, I imagine, quite obsolete called simply the *accordion.* I was much surprised to find that *Grove* (5th edition) makes no mention whatever of the modern instrument (*piano-*accordion), neither do the 1959 **Britannica,** or the **Everyman Encyclopedia of Music** I consulted, and one not familiar with the modern instrument might suppose that the instrument so described (with its limitations) . . . "a mere toy" says Grove . . . was the present-day one. You can see a picture of an old-type accordion in **I See All.**

Only the latest **Chambers** has so far scored on this point. **Collins** states that the accordion was invented by Buschmann of Berlin in 1822. The others (except Chambers) say that it was invented by Damien of Vienna in 1829. Chambers mentions both Buschmann and Damien but is vague about the right-hand button alternative to piano-type keys. None mention that the instrument is specially popular on the Continent.

Somewhat intrigued by this inquiry, I reached for some other "standard" works on the Reference Library shelves. **The Harvard Dictionary of Music** gave a very cursory mention of a "modern" accordion and seemed to imply that the *concertina* (who sees one nowadays?) was the latest thing! An index-reference to *accordion* in Sachs **History of Musical Instruments** was unrewarding. Geiringer's **Musical Instruments** treated the subject as in Grove, etc. The **Macmillan Encyclopedia of Music,** was one of the few which gave a brief reference directly under *Piano Accordion*. The **International Cyclopedia of Music** gave a brief mention.

Later I looked up, at home, one of my favourite reference books, **The Oxford Companion to Music,** and found that its treatment of *Piano-Accordion* was quite good. Here I learnt that the *piano-accordion* was invented by Bouton of Paris in 1852.

You must not think that I am a special pleader for this instrument (one which I play as a change from the pianoforte). I instance the foregoing to show that anyone knowing little about the instrument and looking in the first book to hand might be seriously misdirected. The same could well apply to other subjects. Therefore, verify your references. *Double-check them! Triple-check* if necessary!

Mention must be made of an outstanding reference work—**Encyclopedia of the Social Sciences** (15 vols.)—the first comprehensive work of its kind. It covers political science, economics, Law, penology, etc., and the social aspects of ethics, education, medicine, and the like. It was prepared under the auspices of ten Learned Societies of the U.S.A. and is international in scope. The articles are by named specialists. There is a good deal of biography material, especially where it concerns the subject's achievements in the social sciences.

The various Harmsworth encyclopedias, such as the **Universal** or **Household,** are still useful. The present writer still makes good use of the old **Harmsworth Self-Educator** though this was written some years before he was born. Such subjects as musical theory or Latin grammar do not change and even where the subjects *have* changed (as in dressmaking or shopkeeping) they come in handy as historical references.

Do not despise the smaller—more "potted"—encyclopedias. Naturally, if we wanted to know almost everything about a specific matter, we should consult the **Britannica** entry, but usually we require just an outline of our subject, for which purpose the smaller encyclopedias are most handy. This applies to other reference books.

An ever-useful classic is **Pears Cyclopedia.** It contains sections dealing with matters such as Events and People, Human Relations, Scientific Topics, Greek Myths and Legends, Medical Dictionary, an Atlas, Gazetteer, General Information, Sports, Gardening, and much more. Every annual issue contains something new.

Dictionaries

The average layman usually regards the dictionary as a means of finding the correct spelling or meaning of a doubtful word. The research worker knows better. Some dictionaries give such ample definitions that the line of demarcation between a dictionary and an encyclopedia is difficult to fix. Some classical dictionaries, for example, are really encyclopedias, whilst some concise encyclopedias are little more than dictionaries.

One of the best dictionaries is **A New English Dictionary on Historical Principles** (popularly known as "The Oxford Dictionary"), edited by Sir James A. H. Murray, and others. This shows the meaning, etc., of a word, when it was first used in print, and how it is generally used.* The complete dictionary, a multi-volumed affair, is kept only in the larger libraries, but there are also a two-volume **Shorter English Dictionary,** a **Concise,** and a **Pocket Oxford Dictionary.**

Of the many fine dictionaries that exist, only a few can be mentioned here. Among them are: Webster, **New International Dictionary** (of U.S.A. origin); Funk and Wagnell, **New Standard Dictionary;** Professor Wyld, **Universal English Dictionary;** Skeat, W., **Etymological Dictionary; New Century Dictionary** (six vols.).

For desk and home library use there are: **Nuttall's, Cassell's, Chambers's, Odham's,** and others. **Everyman's English Dictionary,** literary in flavour, includes queer words met with in Burns, Shakespeare, Spenser, etc.

Some extraordinary bargains in dictionaries appear in bookshops. See notes on re-hashed encyclopedias, however, as the same warning applies.

There are literally thousands of dictionaries available, covering definitions of the words used in our own language and in foreign

---

* The Transatlantic counterpart is the 4-vol. **A Dictionary of American English on Historical Principles** (University of Chicago Press).

languages; bilingual dictionaries (one can even get a Tibetan–English Dictionary); encyclopedic and etymological dictionaries; dictionaries of terms used in engineering, science, commerce, etc. Then there are those which deal with abbreviations, e.g. **World List of Abbreviations** (of Scientific, Technological and Commercial Organizations).

There are also such things as dictionaries of slang, clichés, rhymes and so on.

Again there are those dealing with synonyms, e.g. **Roget's Thesaurus of English Words and Phrases.** (recently revised and enlarged).

This is a book that every literary person should possess—a comprehensive collection of synonyms, antonyms, associated words, phrases, etc.; a veritable "treasury" (as the word *Thesaurus* connotes) of words classified and arranged for easy reference.

There is also a **Roget's International Thesaurus** which includes Americanisms.

As with Year Books, etc., the field is so vast that the reader is recommended to find out personally what dictionaries are likely to be of most use.

In the appendixes of "popular" dictionaries, one may find lists of foreign phrases, abbreviations, musical terms, pronunciation of proper names, corresponding tables of centigrade and Fahrenheit systems of measurement of temperature, weights and measures, coinage, currency, meanings, of Christian names, and so on, though such matters often form separate works such as Koch, R., **The Book of Signs** (alchemical symbols, different kinds of crosses, etc.).

There are often supplements of words which, whilst not purely slang, have not been officially admitted to the English language—such words as "beano," "Aussies," "wangle," etc.

An article of mine for a dog journal touched on the origin of breed-names (*terrier* from *terra*, earth; *beagle* from the French *beugler*, to bellow or bray, cf. bugle; *basset* from *bas*, meaning *low*, an obvious reference to the animal's short legs, etc.)—all inspired by and grounded on FACTS from my well-thumbed dictionary.

Special reference must be made to English–Foreign language *Technical* Dictionaries. However large a general bilingual dictionary may be, it often lets one down when dealing with up-to-the-minute technical terms.

The expression "deep freeze" is now accepted English (though someone had originally to coin the expression) and now has its standard equivalents in foreign languages. Yet the present writer well remembers the difficulties encountered in one translation bureau when the expression had to be translated into German. The term—

then newly devised—appeared in no existing technical dictionary. One hesitated to translate, simply, *deep* and *freeze*. Time-consuming correspondence with a Continental agent who searched through German Trade magazines resulted in getting three versions of "deep freeze" (none of which, subsequently, proved to be the now accepted term!). And there is every possibility of the expression (in English, as well as in foreign languages) changing in the course of years. One has only to compare some terms used in a technological dictionary published, say, in the 20's, with those in current usage to realize this. Unless, of course, some have already done so, I suggest that publishers issue a yearly supplement of new or changed technical terms.

I suggest that you mistrust (for technical work) those expensive "general" bi-lingual dictionaries that, in giving, say, the Spanish for *gain*, list half a dozen or more terms taken (apparently indiscriminately) from existing dictionaries without seriously attempting to define shades of meaning. For example the Spanish for *gain*, used in television-set design *may* be, but is not necessarily the same as that for financial *gain*.

There are many specialized multi-lingual dictionaries.

A useful series is that of **Elsevier,** whose dictionaries, in six languages (English, French, German, Spanish, Italian, Dutch), cover such subjects as Television, Cinema, Electronics, Rubber, Pharmacy, and Criminal Science (in separate volumes).

CHAPTER VIII

DIRECTORIES AND YEAR BOOKS

IT is difficult to think of any trade, sport, sect, country, interest, etc., which is not covered by a year book or directory issued at frequent intervals. It is quite impossible to do more than indicate the vast field here.

Directories of Directories

Among lists of year books, directories, etc., we may note **Current British Directories—a complete guide to local trade and professional directories of the British Isles,** compiled by G. P. Henderson. I understand that a **Reference Manual of Directories** by the same compiler will eventually cover *all* countries.

The publication of directories is intended to be a profitable commercial undertaking and it is not unusual to find two, three or even more, directories all much alike competing in the same field. Even if he has ample funds and shelf space (a very optimistic supposition!) the average librarian does not relish unnecessary duplication and he has the difficult task of deciding which publication to order. So, if you ask for the *PQR Directory of the Pottery Trades*, do not be put off if you are offered the *XYZ Directory* instead.

A reference librarian skilfully using, say, fifty well-chosen annuals can probably answer more questions from them than a lesser expert with two hundred books. The moral is choose well: use well (and this applies to most reference aids).

In many large reference libraries you may find a label stuck to the front of directories bearing a note to the effect that "This is the current edition. A new edition is expected in . . . . Earlier editions (from . . .) can be seen on application to the inquiry counter." In most public libraries older directories are sent to branch libraries.

General Year Books

The supreme year book is **Whitaker's Almanack,** which contains "an account of astronomical and other phenomena, and a vast amount of information respecting the Government, finances, population, commerce, and general statistics of the various nations of the world." It is well indexed.

Idly turning over the leaves, one comes across, The Roman Calendar, The Provinces of India, The Peerage, Government and Public Offices, The Royal Navy, The Universities, Societies and Institutions, Annual Premiums for Whole Life Assurance, Infant Mortality in various countries, World Trade, Post Office Guide, Railways, Scottish County Officials, Floods, British Health Resorts, Members of Parliament and Ministers (with their salaries and dates of birth), Drama, Films, Broadcasting, Racing Fixtures, Hall Marks on Plate, Professional Fees, hosts of facts, figures, addresses. No other single book contains the proportionate amount of information, and a *current* copy, of course, is essential for *current* needs. The unabridged edition is, naturally, best for research work.

The Daily Mail Year Book is a handy reference book, cheaply priced. It specializes in short articles summing up recent progress in various fields such as National Defence, British Railways, Lawn Tennis, etc., apart from general facts and figures. A useful feature is a thousand short biographies of present-day people often in the news. Although a *current* edition is obviously necessary in checking current addresses, etc., old issues need not be scrapped, as they may be filed to serve as potted histories of bygone years.

A U.S.A. "Whitaker" is **The World Almanac and Encyclopedia and Book of Facts,** published by the *New York World-Telegram*.

See also **Information Please** (U.S.A.). This contains much "popular" information not normally found in year books. Directories and Year Books (or "Annuals" as they are known to librarians) are mentioned in many places in this book apart from this present chapter, e.g. under Current Affairs, Biography, Periodical Publications, Official Publications, and so on.

There are numerous directories for schools (Public and Preparatory: Girls' Schools: Independent Schools, etc.). Others cover medical services (doctors, dentists, nurses, hospitals, etc.). The Armed Forces all have their Lists.

Commercial Directories

Kelly's Directories are also mines of information. The county guides contain, besides information proper to such a work, particulars of local history, topography, crops, churches, their livings, etc. The big towns have their own directories, whilst London boroughs have separate, smaller ones.

There are fine directories issued to cover various trades such as Building, Electricity, Laundry, Stationery, Furnishing, Upholstery, and so on. Here again, these are not entirely plain lists of names and addresses. Kelly's **Directory of Merchants, Manufacturers and**

Shippers, for example, gives useful gazetteer information as well as notes on trade marks, passport regulations, consuls abroad, rules for commercial travellers in other countries, etc.

Telephone Directories, classified trades and alphabetical, for all capital cities and many large towns of the world will be found in some large public libraries. Foreign telephone directories, especially if classified by trades, etc., are often more useful, reliable and up to date than some expensive Commercial Directories of foreign trade, etc.

Business Aids

A large Public Library Reference Room in a big city would contain such useful works as the Industrial Reference Service of the U.S. Department of Commerce and their World Trade in Commodities Series, bulletins of foreign official statistics, many foreign directories (e.g. Thomas's **Register of American Manufacturers** and the French **Annuaire du Commerce,** Didot-Bottin), journals of most British and some foreign Chambers of Commerce, foreign postal guides, cable code books, and such annuals (in addition to some already mentioned) as—

The Stock Exchange Official Year Book.
Directory of Directors.
F.B.I. Register of British Manufacturers.
Sell's Registered Telegraphic Addresses.
Lloyd's Register of Shipping.

"Useful" Books

Reference librarians are constantly asked for formulae, recipes, "how to do it," etc. To answer these queries, books of the following types are useful—

Spon's Workshop Receipts.
Machinery's Handbook (contains a wealth of information and formulae connected with machinery; together with mathematical tables).
Kempe's Engineer's Year Book.
Laxton's and Lockwood's Builders Price Book.
The British Pharmacopœia (and books of the Home Doctor type).
Encyclopedia of Sports, Games and Pastimes.

There are several books which give the layman a general survey of the Law. Typical of these is—**The Universal Home Lawyer.**

It is most essential to refer (for modern legal practice) to a modern book. For example, the Workmen's Compensation Act dealt with in the older books is now to be referred to under the National Health Insurance Acts in the latest books.

Nearly every time I go into a Reference Library and browse round the shelves I find something new.

CHAPTER IX

"OFFICIAL" PUBLICATIONS

EXTREMELY valuable information is to be found in the publications of Her Majesty's Stationery Office, and other official printers. Most people regard these publications as deadly dull, suitable only for stodgy statisticians and economists. A visit to the Sales Office at York House, Kingsway, London, will give the lie to this, even if we do no more than look at the covers of the booklets, which employ the best typographical skill and devices, and are often illustrated in colour. We shall see, too, that the books do not deal only with "official" and weighty matters of government. There are books and papers on Gardening, Goldfish, Careers, Toys, Tailoring, Flea-beetles, Piracy, etc. I suspect that many research workers fight shy of Government publications because they associate such things with Income Tax returns and other extortions.

Stationery Office Publications

At one end of the scale there is the *Highway Code* (over four million sold). At the other end, there are such works as *Horseflies of the Ethiopian Region*. (Number sold . . .?)

Some of the H.M.S.O. publications are advertised in the lay press.

A catalogue of **Government Publications** is issued monthly with an annual cumulation. The index is of especial value. It is instructive merely to glance through it and to note the wide range of subjects published by H.M.S.O.

A most useful (and cheap) brief guide to Official publications is entitled **Published by H.M.S.O.** It is not a complete catalogue (for this, *see* that entitled **Government Publications**) but describes under the following sub-heads, typical H.M.S.O. publications—

Parliamentary Publications
Agriculture, Fisheries and Food
Science and Technology
Finance, Administration and Trade
Health and Welfare
Transport and Travel

Education and Careers
Fine and Applied Art
History and Archaeology
Architecture and Building
Commonwealth and Foreign Affairs
Military and Civil Defence

Government Periodicals (there are over sixty of them).

There is an Appendix on how to buy Government publications: the Catalogue Service (the frequency of publication of various lists, the card index service, etc.), and details of Agency Publications (e.g. those of U.N.O., N.A.T.O., the International Court of Justice, etc.).

Each section of **Published by H.M.S.O.** gives, for further reference, the numbers of the appropriate *Sectional Lists*. Each, of these (numbering upwards of sixty) constitutes a specialized catalogue.

Thus, the section on *Commonwealth and Foreign Affairs* contains further references to Sectional Lists—

> 7. Treaty Series, 1919–1957
> 34. Colonial Office
> 50. Miscellaneous List
> 53. Central Office of Information
> 58. Foreign Office.

If we then look up Sectional List No. 7 we will find (assuming we were interested in Anglo-German relations) numerous references (listed by the year) to various treaties and agreements. For example, we would ruefully find that in 1938 there was a German-U.K. Limitation of Naval Armament agreement. The Cmd. No. is given (5834) and we can obtain a copy for a few pence. Each year an index is published so we need not thumb over long lists. If we look up the Foreign Office sectional list, we will find, naturally, a very full range of non-parliamentary publications on Germany.

See Chapter XI for a further example of H.M.S.O. Sectional Lists.

See also **Government Information and the Research Worker** (a publication of the London University School of Librarianship).

Statistics

Statistics are often of great importance to many people in Public Affairs. The **Monthly Digest of Statistics** is an official British document. It is issued by the Central Statistical Office, which also issues such other publications as **National Income and Expenditure.** The Board of Trade issues **Census of Production** and **Census of Distribution.** Other Government offices issue similar publications and that is why they are mentioned in this present chapter.

See also the **U.N.O. Statistical Year Book** and the **International Labour Office Year Book.** (These are examples only.)

Parliamentary Publications

An excellent survey of "Parliamentary Publications" is given in "**Published by H.M.S.O.**"

Those which chiefly concern the average research worker are—

House of Commons Parliamentary Debates,

House of Lords Parliamentary Debates,

—familiarly known as *Hansard* from the original publisher. Both of these series are issued daily during the session. They are later cumulated and indexed by speaker and by topic. Select "Blue Books" and similar papers are reviewed in *The Times Literary Supplement*. Select Government publications can also be traced in **The English Catalogue** and in **Whitaker's Cumulative Book Catalogue.**

Select Lists of Parliamentary Papers

Professor and Mrs. Ford have produced some useful lists which eliminate much drudgery in going through old files. See their—

Guide to Parliamentary Papers.

Select List of British Parliamentary Papers (1833–99).

Breviate of Parliamentary Papers—a title which is applied to three separate books covering, respectively, the periods: 1696–1934, 1900–1916, 1917–39.

See also Le May, G. H. L., **British Government (1914–53) Select Documents.**

Catalogue of Parliamentary Papers, 1801–1900, with a few of earlier date (with Supplements covering the periods 1901–1910 and 1911–1920). London: P. S. King. Compiled by Jones, Hilda V. (known to librarians as "King's List").

A Century of Diplomatic Blue Books, 1814–1914. Temperley, Harold. Cambridge University Press.

Foreign Office Papers

Foreign Office Papers would be extremely useful to historians and biographers were it not for the rigorous application of, I understand, a fifty-year wait for access to documents—a policy which serious students naturally find irksome.* See, however, the work of Gooch and Temperley for the pre-1914 period, especially the origins of the First World War and **Documents on British Policy,** by the official historians E. L. Woodward and R. Butler, for the period 1919–39, also the publications commissioned by the Royal Institute of International Affairs.

Parliamentary Procedure

Well known to M.P.'s and also to students of parliamentary procedure is—

May, T. E. **A Treatise On the Law, Privileges, Proceedings and Usages of Parliament**—familiarly called "Erskine May" and whilst

* See a *Times* article (19th June, 1963) "Foreign Historians Get First Say."

not official, is, next to the journals of both Houses, regarded as a great authority.

See also **Dod's Parliamentary Companion** and also the more condensed **Vacher's Parliamentary Companion.**

Local Government

The London County Council publish many valuable papers. Other big cities such as Birmingham and Manchester so publish, but many smaller authorities cannot afford to do so and have a few typewritten copies made instead. You will nearly always find one at the local public library, and certainly at the local Town Hall, or equivalent office. Whenever there is any difficulty in getting facts, a Councillor should be approached (*see* Personal Inquiries, Chapter XVIII). For Local Government affairs, a valuable guide is the **Municipal Year Book.** This tells what each local authority has done in the past year as regards open spaces, water supply, roads, etc., and what it proposes doing in the future.

Incidentally much civic information can be found at Head Post Offices e.g. particulars of Health Services, Citizen's Advice Bureau, various addresses, etc.

Foreign Government Papers

Corresponding to the H.M.S.O. **Government Publications** is the **Subject Guide to U.S. Government Publications** and there are monthly and annual catalogues of U.S. Government publications.

A standard source list is—

List of the Serial Publications of Foreign Governments, 1815–1931, edited by Winifred Gregory for the American Council of Learned Societies, American Library Association and National Research Council (1932). This catalogues the publications and indicates where copies may be found in U.S. libraries. Thus if we wish to trace Netherlands law for reports 1831 (in Dutch) we will find that the *Algemeene Versameling van Decisien* for this date is available in the Harvard Law School. An English student in, say, Birmingham or Brighton, might object that this is not very helpful unless, of course, photostatic or microfilm copies are ordered.

The chief use of Gregory to students outside the U.S.A., however, is in identifying series and dates of publication.

Papers of Learned Societies

There are also immense numbers of these, and it is a difficult field to tackle. Often when the paper is tracked down it is far too "advanced" for a layman to understand. These papers, read to a select audience and not, in general, intended for the whole world, epitomize a man's lifetime of experience in a specialized field. The papers sometimes present difficulty to cataloguers, and if they are not easily found in the catalogue, expert help should be asked. As a general rule "Academies," as these societies are called, are listed under the towns wherein they are situated. (*See* Catalogues, Chapter IV, showing how Societies' papers are listed.)

G. W. Cole, in his Index to the **Bibliographical Papers in the Library Association . . . Papers,** observes that, although "hidden away," in learned societies' publications are countless articles, etc., relating to such societies' activities, "these contributions to knowledge . . . can only be ascertained by long and patient research, unless . . . made available by carefully prepared indexes. Such indexes . . . have been prepared, but, alas, too infrequently."

Since these words were written, the situation regarding indexing has improved somewhat.

It would not be out of place to record here a "classic" bibliography: this is the great Reuss, J. D., **Repertorium,** 16 vols., which contains a mass of material classified into sections such as Chemistry, Astronomy, Mathematics, Technology, etc. It is particularly useful for tracing the publications of Learned Societies from the date of their foundation to c. 1800.

Publications of the United Nation's Organization, U.N.E.S.C.O. and F.A.O. are of considerable value. Formerly we had those of the League of Nations. See U.N.E.S.C.O.'s **Bibliographical Services Throughout the World.**

CHAPTER X

BIOGRAPHY, CHARACTERS IN FICTION
AND DATES

IN certain kinds of writing, facts about *people* are accounted of much more interest than, say, facts about imports of sago from Senegal. We are constantly having to refer to biographies to find out who people are, or were, what they have done, are trying to do, etc. We ourselves may even be writing a full-length biography.

Published Biographies

If we wish to find out much about a certain person, we should ascertain whether his or her biography has been published. Biographies vary greatly in treatment. They may be a plain chronicle of events, with a few impartial comments. The book may deal mainly with the subject's influence on certain matters, or connexion with certain people. The book may set out either to "debunk" a popular character, or to vindicate another. One has to reckon on the biographer's bias. Especially in the autobiographies of celebrities, one has to take much of the information with a pinch of salt.

Some subjects have been overdone. On the other hand, biographies have been written around lesser men—country squires, missionaries, eccentrics, thieves, etc. Therefore do not think that only the "big" names have been written about.

Where a subject *is* overdone, do not assume that *everything* has been said about it. Newly-released information may shed a new light on the matter.

Biographies often contain much more than personal data. It is usual to give a survey of general conditions of the period in which the subject lived and the circle he or she moved in. For example, biographies of eighteenth-century M.P.s might give us details of Parliamentary procedure of the time.

Some Techniques in Writing Biography

All interested in biography should read A. J. A. Symons' **The Quest for Corvo.** The book shows how the author first became interested in his subject; how he found press cuttings, letters, etc., and how, gradually, he became acquainted with persons who had known "Baron Corvo." Here is a fact-finder in action.

Other biographers sometimes give hints on how they obtained

some of their *first-hand* material as (in a quite random example) Robert Standish in his biography of Phillips Oppenheim (**The Prince of Storytellers**).

See also in this present book (Chapter XXI) a reference to Hesketh Pearson.

Although, as we shall soon see, there are annuals devoted to the biography of members of a certain profession or class (e.g. **The Jewish Who's Who**) it sometimes pays better to look up (in a guide to reference material) the profession first (say Chemistry) and, then refer to biographical material in this, e.g. Smith, H. M. **Torchbearers of Chemistry** (brief biographies of scientists who have contributed to the making of modern chemistry).

Biographical Dictionaries

For quick reference, a large number of biographical dictionaries have been compiled, whilst the Library Association have issued an **Analytical Bibliography of Universal Collected Biography,** comprising books published in English in Great Britain and Ireland, the U.S.A., and the British Dominions.

The following are some standard works—

The Dictionary of National Biography (edited originally by Sir Leslie Stephen and Sidney Lee).

People in every walk of life are included : saints, sinners, statesmen, sportsmen, soldiers, sailors, bishops, and burglars. The epithet "National" is taken to include early American colonists of British stock, and foreigners who achieved some distinction in this country. Living people are not included.

After the various accounts appear details of other references, and particulars of the subject's own literary works (if any) and where portraits may be found.

Though you may well find the older editions (especially of the earlier series) in some libraries, the present edition spans the following periods. (*a*) From the earliest times to 1900: 22 volumes (some 30,000 names); (*b*) 1901–11: 3 volumes in 1; (*c*) 1912–21; (*d*) 1922–30; (*e*) 1931–40; (*f*) 1941–50 . . . i.e. the **Twentieth Century D.N.B.** volumes cover ten-year periods. When the Dictionary first started, the compilers obviously had to rely on written records for details of long dead people, but in the later volumes, the writers have based their contributions on first-hand intimate knowledge of the subjects. Thus the Lives are authoritative and often entertaining reading.

There is also a **Concise D.N.B.** (*a*) From the beginnings to 1900; (*b*) 1901–50. This abridged edition is appreciated, not only for its reduced cost and bulk (an important consideration in the home-library), but also because it furnishes us with a means of quick reference. All libraries worthy of their name ought at least to have a Concise edition. The original Dictionary, of course, appeals largely to students of bygone history, whereas the Twentieth Century volumes appeal to the student of more recent and contemporary events and persons.

Particular mention has been made of this great Dictionary because it is the largest of all national biographies and without rival. The present publishers are the Oxford University Press, who also issue the **Dictionary of American Biography** of which eleven volumes and an index have been published.

Other countries have their national bibliographies (such as the **Allgemeine Deutsche Biographie.**) For those countries which have no reliable national Who's Who the **International Who's Who** is useful.

Boase, Frederick, **Modern English Biography,** 6 vols., 3 original, 3 supplements (1892–1921), includes short, but exact, notes on many lesser lights deceased since 1850, and an interesting index, where, instead of looking under particular names, we can reverse the process and look up , say, *Pugilists*, or *Seamen Tried for Piracy*. Consulting "Fancy Names," we can discover the identity of *Finality Jack*, or *Jim the Penman*.

Reference librarians find quite useful the series of biographical dictionaries (of literary figures) by Kunitz and Haycraft and Chambers's newly revised **Dictionary of Biography** is also very well thought of.

Who's Who is the well-known annual dealing in a nutshell with outstanding contemporary Britons and a few distinguished foreigners. It gives details of their addresses, clubs, education, works, recreations, etc.

Who Was Who contains the pick of past volumes of *Who's Who*, and thus bridges the gap between the current *Who's Who* and the older standard national biographies.

See also **Current Biography,** monthly and cumulating annually.

Biography Index. A U.S.A. work. H. W. Wilson Co. Deals mostly with U.S. citizens.

As *examples* only of the wealth of specialized biography, covering all trades and professions, old established and newly-arrived, we might mention—

Who's Who in the Theatre (Pitman).

Who's Who in Show-Business.

The Authors' and Writers' Who's Who.

A **Dictionary of Literary Biography** (Everyman's Reference Library).
A **Dictionary of Art and Artists** (Penguin).
The Catholic Who's Who.
Law List.
Medical Directory.

And do not forget that such year books as **Whitaker's Almanack** give lists of public officials and, often, brief biographies.

Foreign and Overseas Biography

Corresponding to the English **Who's Who,** we have such works as—

Qui Êtes-vous?   ¿Quién es Quién?
Wer ist Wer?   Chi È.
Who's Who In America. (Biennially, with monthly supplements).
Who's Who in Canada (China, Latin America, etc.).
See also **World Biography** (a U.S.A. publication).

The above are quoted as examples. There are dozens of others. Inquire of the librarian which are stocked.

The Aristocracy, etc.

There are several publications, among them **Burke's Peerage, Baronetage and Knightage, Debrett's Peerage, Baronetage Knightage and Companionage** (various volumes), **Dod's Peerage,** and **Whitaker's Peerage, Royal Blue Book, Royal Red Book,** etc.

It is thus quite easy for a foreigner to check up on British titles, but it is not so easy for us to differentiate between genuine foreign nobility and the host of bogus Counts, Barons, Marquises, and other Ruritanian rascals. There are, at present, few reference books on European aristocracy and such classic guides as **Almanach de Gotha** and **Ruvigny** grow yearly more outdated. But *see* **World Nobility and Peerage.**

Characters in Fiction

Is is often desired to find out who, for example, Becky Sharp was, who created her, and in what book. One work which tells us is Walsh, Wm. S., **Heroes and Heroines of Fiction.** Others are: Braybrooke, P., **Great Children in Literature,** and Conne, **Dictionary of the Characters in H. G. Wells's Works.** These are typical.

Various

No single work could treat universal biography, ancient and modern, with any degree of completeness.

Hyamson, A. D., **Dictionary of Universal Biography.**

This gives the names of all the persons to be found in a large selection of major biographical dictionaries that are identified in each case by letter key. The subjects, with birth and death dates, are themselves briefly identified on the principle of "one person, one line" thus—

Clive, Rob., 1st Bar., Gov. of Bengal, 1725–44. A:D:O:V

The key letters here indicate that Clive has entries in the **Dictionary of National Biography; Dictionary of Indian Biography; Nouvelle Biographie Universelle;** and the **Encyclopaedia Britannica.**

Chambers' **Biographical Dictionary** is to be found in many libraries as a standard reference work.

Lippincott's **Pronouncing Dictionary of Biography and Mythology** is a U.S.A. book, but international in scope. As the name suggests, the pronunciation of the various names is one of the features of this book—no easy matter when one has to include names of all nations and tongues. It must be noted, generally, that U.S. pronunciation is not always the same as English.

For the use of their news-readers and the like, broadcasting stations maintain a list of current pronunciations of personal and place names, in addition to a general list of "Broadcast English." These pronunciations do not always please the purists but they are better than improvisations. Those who have much public speaking to do, involving the pronunciations of foreign names and places might do well to inquire, from radio and T.V. stations whether lists of pronunciations are available.

A modern edition of an established book is **A New Century Cyclopedia of Names—in Geography, Biography, Mythology, History, Ethnology, Art, Architecture, Fiction, etc.** (to quote the sub-title).

All encyclopedias of a general nature, and many year books, include biographical information.

"Paste-up" Biographies

The larger newspapers have elaborate files of information and it is fairly common knowledge that one man, at least, is almost permanently employed in pasting up "dossiers" of press cuttings and other data relating to the Famous so that when one dies, or if, as the *Observer* calls them, a "Profile" or the like is required, a complete biographical file is immediately to hand. This practice is adopted by alert-minded compilers of various *Who's Who* type of reference books.

The writer who specializes in personalia can work similarly. Much of the success in this line comes from spotting the *potentially* famous and starting the file whilst the subject is only *just* becoming known. Incidentally, on occasion, we may look up out-of-date year books to trace the rise of a now famous person. What was his "rating" say, five years ago?

Full-length biographies appear nowadays almost before the subject is cold in his grave. Formerly the Great may have piously wondered what the Recording Angel had written in his book. Today, they must wonder what their confidential secretaries (and other writers) have got in the dossier.

Local newspapers usually give ample space to local celebrities who have just died, or who have retired or have received Honours or the like . . . information which might be ignored in the National newspapers or dismissed, in a few lines, in a professional journal.* If, therefore, you know, within a few weeks or so, when your subject was strong "local" news, the local newspaper is the place to look.

Some personal information which the Famous withhold from a "popular" directory is often divulged in a more specialist professional directory. Occasionally the reverse can happen. Details of salaries paid to public servants should be public knowledge and are therefore given in such reference books as **Whitaker's Almanack** whereas they might be considered vulgarly ostentatious if given in a specialist directory.

Bogus Biography

Be on your guard against biographical material that eulogizes a subject in the expectation that he will subscribe to the work or take out advertising space therein. With experience and a modicum of wordly wisdom you can smell out such suspect material. To gather material, some editors send out questionnaires to the prospective biographees. Some prospects are not averse to self-praise and *some* publishers are uncritical.

On the other hand—as with **Who's Who**—it is impossible to recommend yourself for inclusion, let alone buy your way into some reference books.

Dates

As a general rule, it is much quicker to resort to standard historical and biographical works to ascertain dates than look to up the matter in various dictionaries of dates with their thousands of entries. These dictionaries are very useful if one wishes to find out, for example, all the important events of 1872, or what centenaries happen to be due.

* The *Times* obituary notices are not confined to "top people" in the learned professions but cover a wide range of people who were before the public eye.

On the other hand, if one wishes to know when Oliver Cromwell was born, it is usually better to look up a standard biography.

Some reference books are specially recommended by reviewers as being useful in checking dates, e.g. C. M. Woodhouse's **British Foreign Policy since the Second World War.**

Haydn's Dictionary of Dates and Universal Information. Here we have a kind of encyclopedia, where the emphasis is laid on the *dates*. Thus, among other information on the first page, we are told the *date* when Aalesund was destroyed by fire, the *date* when the Abacus was developed, and *dates* relative to Abbeys. Under such entries as Fires, Trials, and Wrecks, lengthy lists are provided. Under the headings of various nations, a chronological list of chief events in their history is given. An old work, still useful (up to 1910).

See also Helen Rex Keller's **Dictionary of Dates** and also Steinberg, S. H., **Historical Tables** (58 B.C.–A.D. 1945).

In the **Dictionary of Dates** (Everyman's Library) "the aim . . . has been to give every date likely to be of service to the general reader while getting rid of the superfluities which make the typical date book too bulky for easy use."

Little, C. E., **Cyclopedia of Classified Dates** is a very useful work, especially for speedy reference. The book is first divided into sections dealing with individual countries such as Abyssinia, France, Russia, etc., and each of these sections is sub-divided into standardized sub-headings dealing with Army, Navy, Church, State, Births, Deaths, Society, and a few others. Thus if we wish to trace the earliest Church affairs of Turkey, or the army affairs of Rumania round about 1800, we can do so at once. Likewise we can trace the development of Spanish literature independently of other matters. There is an index of remarkable completeness.

See also **Newnes Dictionary of Dates and Anniversaries** compiled by Robert Collison.

For fairly *recent* dates *see Current Affairs* (Chapter XV).

CHAPTER XI

SCIENCE AND TECHNOLOGY

IT should be appreciated that whilst this chapter deals specifically with many sources of information relevant to scientific and technological matters, it is not complete in itself. It is necessary to read the *whole* of the book, where such other matters as general library routine, the use of bibliographies, catalogues and booklets, technical dictionaries, the finding of articles in back numbers of periodicals, efficient note-taking, and the like, are dealt with. Conversely those whose interests are far from scientific are also urged to study this present chapter as many of the remarks applying to science matters can often be paralleled for some other subjects.

The Technical Writer

Since this book was first written, the profession of the technical writer has shown remarkable and continuing development. The technical *writer* is not necessarily the same as a technical or trade *journalist* or *reporter*. The technical writer is usually on the full-time staff of a manufacturing firm and is employed mainly to gather information from the firm's research workers (a science genius is very often a halting exponent of clear English!); from engineers, engineer reporters, drawing offices, user-reports and the like, and to present it in the form of clearly written (and illustrated) bulletins, instruction leaflets, instruction manuals, and so on, for the benefit of the firm's customers, actual or potential.

A well-known electronics firm took out advertising space to announce—

Every year the Mullard laboratories and technical information departments issue hundreds of different publications. They include detailed laboratory and application reports, catalogues and libraries of technical data, pamphlets, information sheets, newsletters and magazines. In addition, Mullard authors contribute articles to technical journals and Mullard scientists and engineers lecture to designers, users and servicers of electronic equipment.

This unique information service is one of the more important contributions to progress in electronics today. Besides providing guidance in the best and most economic use of electronic valves, tubes, semiconductors and magnetic components it helps to keep designers up to date with the most advanced developments and trends in electronic circuitry.

All this information is freely available.

The technical writer, as such, is usually "fed" on facts by research and other departments and his skill, apart from fully understanding what it is all about, comes in sifting and in presenting this information. A selection of reference books and the reading of appropriate technical magazines, catalogues, and the like, connected with the industry concerned, helps fill in background facts where required.

The Technical Report

The research worker, writing a technical report, is in a different position. He is usually engaged in seeking some new development or extended application of an existing idea. Many practical experiments are necessary and apart from his basic knowledge (many research workers being Science Graduates) he has usually read up something of what has already been written on the subject of his specialized research.

Granted always that the mere reading about what other men have done is in industry no substitute for doing some practical research work of one's own, experience shows that *in all too many cases the research man has not read enough.* A firm with an inefficient research department could spend hundreds—or even thousands—of pounds on an apparently "new," semi-secret development only to find that almost identical information could have been obtained for the price of a few shillings-worth of photo-copies of an article which appeared in certain technical journals (possibly of limited, highly-specialized circulation) a few years ago. It is not very clever to get the firm's amateur linguist (at the cost of the wages involved) to translate an involved article from a German magazine, or to pay heavily for a professional (whose ability to deal with technical terms you must often take on trust) to translate a Russian language agriculture-machinery report only to find that D.S.I.R. or ASLIB (*see* notes to come) possibly have these already expertly translated and available, for little more than the nominal price of making a copy.

Industrial Libraries

So far as *books* are concerned, the technical writer will, of course, have his own collection of standard reference books. As an example of the many fine modern reference works for science and industry, I instance Pitman's **Encyclopedic Dictionary of Electronics and Nuclear Science.** Such established publications as **Kempe's Engineer's Year Book** are well known and **Van Nostrand's Science Dictionary** is typical of those useful for quick reference. For new books see **Technical Book Review** and further on in this chapter under ASLIB Services.

Hansom Books currently issue a monthly **Technical Book Guide** and **Technical Books-In-Print.**

An industrial firm of any importance ought to have its own properly-run reference library. Such organizations as ASLIB will be pleased to advise members on the setting up and maintenance of such a library.*

The resources of the local public library should not be disdained. Some highly technical works are often in stock and practically any book can be obtained. Lewis's Library can be useful.

Patent Office Library

The doyen of all science libraries in this country (and possibly in the world) is that of the Patent Office Library, two minutes' walk from Chancery Lane (Underground) Station, London. It is hoped that it will form the basis of a projected National Reference Library for Science and Invention. Quite two thousand readers a week use it. Some are regulars, usually employed by the Patent Agents who mostly have their offices nearby. Spare-time research workers in London who are at other work during the day will be glad to know that the Patent Office Library is currently open until 9 p.m. on weekdays (Saturdays until 1 p.m.) No Permit or Reader's Ticket is required. One simply signs a visitor's book and leaves one's brief-case, or the like, with the cloakroom attendant. There are, in this library, approximately 375,000 volumes, with a great number of pamphlets and trade catalogues, arranged on open-access shelves. The periodical titles currently received number about 7,000 and date from 1855. There is, naturally, a great collection of U.K. Patent Publications and cognate official records and also Commonwealth, U.S.A. and other available foreign ones.

British Abstracts of Patent Specifications form a valuable science and technical source-material. See Mathys, H., **Patents As a Source of Information** (Aslib Proceedings. 4,2,69 1951). A list of **Illustrated Abridgements of Specifications** can be obtained from the Patent Office Library. Besterman in his **Bibliography of Bibliographies** lists certain Patents sources.

A weekly *Journal* issued by the Patent Office gives a list of titles and, by giving a standing order to the Librarian, a firm can receive copies of Patent specifications relating to a subject in which it is interested. To make a thorough search through all relevant Patents on a certain subject (and this requires some experience) one must visit the Patent Office personally or engage the services of one of the many Agents who specialize in this kind of work.

* See also the Library Association's **Scientific Books Libraries and Collectors** and also their **Library Science Abstracts.**

A fully descriptive leaflet (**Guide to the Use of the Library**) is obtainable gratis whilst an article on the Patent Library appeared in the **Library World** for June 1960.

There is a privately-published weekly **Patents Abstracts Journal.**

The Science Museum Library at South Kensington is another fine place for research. **The Weekly List of Accessions** is very useful.

Trade Catalogues and Booklets

In science and technology, however, books date very rapidly except, possibly, those dealing with basic knowledge. Current information is to be had from appropriate periodicals and the like. No research worker should ever assume that because a thing is published in a bulky "hard-back" inevitably expensive volume, it is necessarily more valuable than a free, pamphlet-like publication. Often the reverse is the case. Indeed, in a well-run library, Trade Catalogues are carefully filed.

These range from single sheets, through booklets of all sizes, up to great volumes the size of a Family Bible. In order to raise them from the ranks of mere lists and prices—to be thrown away when outdated—enterprising sales managers incorporate many pages of most useful technical information, tables, diagrams, etc. Thus, if we are looking for certain proportions, dimensions, weights, etc., of, say, special-purpose iron pipes, and cannot easily find the information in the usual reference books, we may find it in the catalogue of one of the biggest pipe manufacturers. The present writer, for example, visited Sheffield to write up some articles on how tools, old and new, were made. For the modern tools he naturally visited several factories but for details of old tools and methods he inquired at the head public library there and was shown several old catalogues, carefully filed. These contained exactly the information he wanted.

The catalogues, if kept in the home library, should be numbered and dated and an index made. The smaller pamphlets can be stored in small box files made for the purpose. Although it has no direct reference to Science, one may note that a classic example of a catalogue becoming a reference book is that of a stamp dealer's catalogue (e.g. **Gibbons**).

As an example of the catalogue-cum-reference book we have the six volume **Architects' Standard Catalogue.** The catalogue pages are specially prepared for this work in standard format. Additionally there is much technical information of various aspects of building and design: notes on relevant Laws; a bibliography of useful H.M.S.O., etc., publications, a directory of builders, a list of brand names . . . and much else.

If you are a technical writer, be ever on the look-out for publications issued by the development boards of various trades. The present writer, searching for facts on the manufacture of tin-cans, was given, free, a bulletin of the International Tin Research and Development Council. In case the word "bulletin" should conjure up visions of a small pamphlet, it should be explained that this bulletin contained 145 pages, well illustrated, quarto size. In fact, if the bulletin was bound up like an ordinary book, it would be worth paying about a guinea for. Not all such publications are so large but all are worth getting.

Mention might be made here of the **Vertical File Index** (U.S.A.). This is an annotated and classified subject list (with title, author, publisher, price, etc.) of such material as pamphlets, booklets, brochures and the like—often unabashed advertising or propaganda—which, whilst often falling outside the scope of conventionally-acquired library stock is, nevertheless, of considerable value.

General Science Periodicals and Books

Apart from specialist trade and professional journals many technicians take in such publications as the **Scientific American: Nature: Discovery: The Times Science Review** (and also the **Review of Industry**) and **The New Scientist** to name a few.

For the *general* reader, the National Book League's bibliography **Science for All** is useful. This is an annotated list of over 700 books on the physical and biological (excluding medicine) and on natural history. Originally issued in 1958, it is kept up to date by multi-graphed annual supplements.

The catalogues of Technical Booksellers are often well worth studying.

Trade Journals

The edition of *Willings* (*see* Chapter XV) before me, lists quite fifty journals in some way connected with radio and television. Only a few people need go through them all. Even an elementary analysis, working on the mere titles alone without reference to the actual contents shows that some of the magazines are for the layman and some for the professional. The title "Audio-Visual Selling" is self-explanatory. The layman magazines might be divided into those which are, in effect, annotated programmes (such as the *Radio Times*) and those which are for the amateur constructor and experimenter. The professional and Trade magazines can further be classified (still roughly) into those of interest chiefly to theorists; to manufacturers; to shopkeepers; to advertising men, and so on. Even where two journals seem somewhat alike, it will be found that each has its specialities: one Radio and TV traders' magazine might be strong on information regarding the servicing of customers' purchases: another might be strong on business-getting ideas.

Those in the "Trade" soon get to know which of the more usual journals prove the most useful though in most offices the routine of circulating the journals and, afterwards, storing them, after extracting and filing useful information, is woefully primitive. It can be safely presumed that the circulation departments of Trade magazines bring their productions to the notice of firms not yet subscribing.

Professional Journals

But there are many erudite Journals, Proceedings of Learned and Professional Societies, and the like, which are not so often seen by the average research man. See, for example, the **World List of Scientific Publications** (published by Butterworth) where we have such titles as *Acta Gnathologica:* the *Bulletin of the Hawaiian Volcano Research Association:* the various *Publications of the Szeged University:* the *Journal de Mal de Mer:* the *Journal of Small Animal Practice* and so on. This book is a most valuable reference tool as it lists about 50,000 scientific technical periodicals and indicates where the majority of them can be found in about 250 British libraries.

The Foreign Books Department of the leading booksellers . . . and especially those in university cities . . . will ascertain which journals cover your subject and will obtain for you any scientific, technical or medical book or periodical published anywhere in the world.

But if one plods through six trade journals a week the odds are that you have missed information in another six . . . or sixty . . . (or even six hundred taken on a world-wide basis). How can you be sure that the latest Paper (or even one published in 1937 and subsequently neglected and forgotten) published by the Tasmanian Trigonometrical Society doesn't contain the "missing link" of information you need on Waveform Generator theory?

Science and Technology are well-documented subjects. As we learn from our earliest entry to the school "lab," we have not only to make practical experiments but have to record them most methodically. The notebooks of Leonardo da Vinci and of Faraday (to name, at random, two well-known scientists), still set an example to modern research men. There seems to be an unwritten law among scientists that no new knowledge can remain hidden but must be communicated to other scientists. Contrary to the average layman's hasty conception, the purpose of a Patent is not to keep new developments secret but to *reveal* them and to make them contribute eventually to the country's industrial well-being. To encourage this revelation the developers are given the means of harvesting the first fruits of their labours.

Provided he gets due credit for being first with the discovery, the average scientist is only too pleased to pass on the results of his investigations. When being interviewed for higher posts, candidates are often asked "What have you had published?" and, in an advertisement appealing for science graduates to join a certain Government research station, one notes the inducement: "Good opportunities offered for the writing and publication of suitable Papers." It is, indeed, an honour, not lightly gained (or sustained) to be asked to read a Paper before a Professional Society and only the real specialist with something important to say can get his writings into the professional journals.

The theses submitted by University candidates for higher degrees are expected to contain original research work, and, as such, are valuable to other research workers. The larger and more specialized libraries have copies (or will have copies made) of the more important English theses, together with (for example) abstracts of U.S.A. Dissertations and French Doctorial theses.

The *kudos* attached to "What have you had published?" seems also to apply to *countries*. Whilst we should not be so foolish as to ignore the actual scientific value of the many well-produced English-languge Abstracts (on technical subjects) put out by Iron Curtain countries, we should not be so naïve as to overlook the propaganda purpose.

All this material: reports from Research Stations, articles in technical magazines, Papers read before Societies, Bulletins from Trade sources . . . and much else, pours in a mighty torrent. It rapidly "dates" and is constantly replenished. How is one to keep up with it?

Abstracts and Digests

The problem is not so difficult as it might at first appear, thanks to the now extensive publication of Abstracts and Digests. Provided you are a specialist (and specialization begins at school nowadays) you can, in "capsule" form, receive regular details of world-wide developments within your specialization and if any of these "capsule" notices (which can be filed) warrant fuller investigation you can read the complete thing.

Whether there is a *strictly applied* difference between *Abstracts* and between *Digests* I am not prepared to say. Typical of the English published digests we have the well-known *Engineers' Digest*. As with most of its kind it is typographically bright whilst losing none of its intrinsic value. In addition to the publication of relatively longer digests of articles appearing in, say, the foreign technical press, there are, in this journal, such features as the "Mini-Digest" and the "Quick Glance at the Latest Technical Developments Throughout the World." The Digest is sub-titled "World Review of Research and Production: Research and Development."

We also have (another typical example) the *Medical Digest*. Over a wider field we have *European Technical Digests*. There are also, for further a example, the *Technical Digests of the E.P.A.*

A *Digest* is, I should say, a condensed version of an article, keeping, as far as possible, to the author's own phrasing. Publication seems to imply that it has passed a "Selection Committee," so to speak, and was picked from many other "candidates." For the general reader, the Editorial staffs of technical journals and the individual contributors perform a valuable service in making significant selections from the mass of information available. But opinions naturally vary as to what *is* significant.

Abstracts are short *summaries* of an article which, in itself, may be lengthy and erudite. Abstracts are rarely—and preferably should not be—criticisms, and the abstractor does not venture to weigh up the merits of the subject of his abstract. One gets the impression that an Abstract is offered as technical news. But we will not argue on "dictionary" definitions or current use (or misuse) of *digest* and *abstract*.

As an example of an Abstract, the following (quoted with acknowledgement from *Hungarian Technical Abstracts*) may be cited. I have chosen it because although the Abstract is in English, the original—details of the source of which precede the Abstract—was in Russian. This gives rise to the question: is an English translation of the whole unabridged article available? (We will deal with this soon.)

Production of heat-treated alloyed aluminium wires for conductors

Experiments were carried out in order to investigate the effect of production methods on Aldrey-type alloyed aluminium wires. Ageing after hardening or before cold working proved to have an important and advantageous effect on the properties of the material. Further investigations showed that the iron content of the alloy has a considerable effect on electric resistance and less influence on the mechanical strength of the material.

Very useful and well known in science libraries is the monthly **Science Abstracts** issued by the Institute of Electrical Engineers in association with the Physical Society, the Institute of Physics, the American Physics Society and the American Institute of Electrical Engineering. Section A deals with Physics and the separately-issued Part B deals with Electrical Engineering. The parts are also issued printed on one side of the page only so that various items can be cut out and pasted up for card-indexing. (Classification is by U.D.C.)

Specialized Abstracts relating to telecommunications (from **Electronic and Radio Engineering**) are reproduced in the *Proceedings of the Institute of Radio Engineers*.

From U.N.E.S.C.O. (obtainable through H.M.S.O.) comes a bilingual (English and French) world-wide bibliography of bibliographies —**Index Bibliographicus** in two volumes. (1) Science; (2) The Humanities.

This, in sub-headings arranged according to the U.D.C. Classification, lists bibliographies, abstracting journals, and the journals of Learned and Professional Societies, etc. The issue before me is not very recent but one hopes that a new edition will eventually appear, to maintain the undoubted usefulness of this work.

Abstracts are available for many science subjects and many industries. At random I instance those for Biology, Cheese, Chemistry, Forestry, Horticulture, Gelatine and Glue, Nuclear Science, Plastics, Textiles and for Tobacco. The existence of such Abstracts can often be established from the catalogue of a good science library. Those actually in Industry will usually have the existence of such publications brought to their attention by their professional organizations.

The D.S.I.R. (*see* notes to come) issue a large number of single-sheet *Technical Digests*, pointing out noteworthy items in the current technical press.

Various journals publish Abstracts. The Royal Society has issued a **List of Periodicals and Bulletins (published in Great Britain) containing Abstracts**. The Royal Society's Information Services Committee has also issued a **List of British Scientific Publications Reproducing Original Work or Critical Reviews**. There is a subject index so that we can discover which journal publishes (sometimes as a summary) work on, say, the chemistry of oils and colours.

Some big business organizations sponsor (for prestige reasons, one presumes) certain Abstracting Services. To instance a U.S.A. example, Eastman Kodak provide a useful series of *Photography Abstracts*.

It seems reasonable to assume that only journals of the highest standing are handled by the best Abstracting Services and these journals are certain to check the qualifications of their contributors.

By the use of such abstracts a technician is saved the almost impossible task of reading (or even skimming over) a huge (and expensive) pile of journals weekly in the hope that there *may* be something of direct professional interest to him.

Abstracting Services

There are various commercial Abstracting Services which may be employed. For example, there is the Technical Information Service of Washington D.C. Another, the Engineering Index Service of New York issues as an annual volume or in posted weekly batches of index cards, very short Abstracts, about 50,000 a year in some 300 subject divisions, taken from about 2,000 journals from all over the world. It is possible to subscribe to any of the sections. The cost of each single card seems reasonable enough but in well-documented subjects the total cost can rapidly mount up. Yet to those who like the convenience of the cards and want to miss nothing of technical developments as well as economic, legal and patent, etc., matters, in their trade, the cost is usually well repaid.

Ulrich lists various Abstracting Services (*see* Chapter XV).

The amount (and quality) of scanning done by various Abstracting Services and in different subjects varies.

Technical Periodical Indexes

Though the various digest and abstracting journals cover, between them, a large number of journals ranging over a large number of fields it is often useful to have, in addition, an index to a selected number of technology journals.

A U.S.A. work, much used in English libraries is the H. W. Wilson Co.'s *Applied Science and Technology Index*, (formerly the *Industrial Arts Index*) a subject index to a selected list of engineering periodicals.

Trade and Business periodicals are now covered by the *Business Periodicals Index.*

The Bell Telephone Company promotes, in the U.S.A., a semi-monthly *Index To Current Technical Literature.* Part of this consists of facsimile reproductions of the contents tables of technical magazines (a practice, also, of the *Index Information Service*, published in the U.S.A.).

Formerly there was the IOTA (Index Of Technical Articles) Service. Now the Library Association fill the gap with a *British Technology Index.* Over a third of the 450 titles are not indexed elsewhere.

I note, at the same time, the establishment of the Derwent Information Service (for Patents, Abstracts, etc.). The author of an

Observer article on Science was announced as Director of Science Information Service.

Bibliographies

As a whole chapter (V) has been written on *Bibliographies*, it will be sufficient to instance here, as typical examples, only a few relating to science matters.

Librarians in Government-Office or Government-Aided libraries bring out numerous bibliographies. Again, as a random example, I instance the *References to Barium Titanate* issued by the Admiralty Centre for Scientific Information and Liaison. From the British Council Science Library comes, for example, *Some References to Brucellosis in Great Britain from* 1950. The National Coal Board has its Scientific Department Records Section, whilst the Science Museum *Bibliographical Series* are well known and esteemed. All these can be seen in a large Science library or obtained through ASLIB or other inter-library services.

The Library Association is, as usual, well to the fore with its Special Subjects List on, for example, Rubber, Radio Astronomy, Control Equipment. The aim is to show all sources of information on such subjects.

H.M.S.O. Publications on Science and Technology

A general description of H.M.S.O. publications is given in Chapter IX. We will deal here with those concerned with the subject of the present chapter.

Typical Sectional Lists of interest to scientists and technologists are—

No. 3. Department of Scientific and Industrial Research (which includes the National Physics Laboratory).
8. Aeronautical Research Council.
12. Medical Research Council.
14. Electricity Division, Ministry of Power.
15. Air Ministry.
61. Building.
63. Atomic Energy.

This is by no means a complete list since, for example, the Ministry of Supply has published a report on *Plastics*, e.g. "Cast Acrylic Sheet in the Tropics." The Ministry of Works has published one on "Dampness in Buildings" and the Ministry of Housing and Local Government one on "Synthetic Detergent."

If we consult No. 3 (above) we will find, first, a list of Research and other establishments of D.S.I.R. (e.g. those concerned with Building,

Fire, Fuel Hydraulics, Mineral Processing, Water Pollution, etc.) and then, under these, a list of publications emanating from each. For example we can get from the Building Research Station a special report (written for industry) on "Mobile Tower Cranes for Two and Three Story Building"; a bulletin dealing in a practical way with "Bonding New Concrete to Old," or a research paper of interest to those engaged in development work on, say, "Sound Insulation between Dwellings." There are details of the monthly *Building Science Abstracts* and (also monthly) *Building Research Station Digests* (notes on selected topics, e.g. "The Causes of Dampness in Buildings" prepared in a form most suitable for practical application).

And so it goes on with publications of other research stations. If you were concerned with, for example, the durability of concrete you could hardly claim to be well read in the subject until you had read all the publications on the matter issued by the D.S.I.R. (There are, of course, other research stations run by some other industries, outside the Government scheme.)

And thus, also, with other technical and scientific subjects, as, for instance, Medicine. The above have been given as examples only. It is quite unnecessary to go into further detail since this would involve duplicating the official H.M.S.O. catalogues (which are inexpensive enough).

By a simple coding (A, B or C), indication is given whether the papers are for the expert specialist; for the moderately experienced, or for the intelligent layman. For specialists it is useful to know that on receipt of a standing order, all publications relating to a certain subject (a list is available from H.M.S.O.) can be sent as soon as they are issued.

From D.S.I.R. one can obtain (free) the useful publications—**Just An Idea** (using new ideas in Industry). **Combining for Research** (the work of the Industrial Research Associations in the Government Scheme) and **Research At Your Service.** A new National Lending Library for Science and Technology has been established by the Department of Scientific and Industrial Research at Boston Spa, Yorks. It will eventually contain millions of volumes and provide industrial firms, research organizations, universities and technical colleges and Government departments with a loan and photographic copy service for scientific literature.

Foreign Technical Reports

The "opposite numbers" of H.M.S.O. in many foreign countries issue technology reports. Those from the U.S.A. are specially valuable. For example, from the Office of Technical Services, U.S.

Dept. of Commerce comes a monthly *U.S. Government Research Reports Available To Industry*.

Corresponding to our own Patent Office *Official Journal* is the weekly *U.S. Patent Office Journal Gazette* with annual index.

See also the *Technical Book Review Index* (U.S.A.).

Unless you are sure of your way about foreign sources, however, it might be as well to subscribe to one of the Abstracting Services.

ASLIB

Manufacturing and marketing companies who are setting up their own research departments would be well advised to get information about ASLIB (short for the Association of Special Libraries and Information Bureaux). Its command of specialized technical information on scientific industrial and commercial matters is almost unrivalled and if adequate use is made of its many services one soon recoups, with interest, the annual subscription (which even in the case of manufacturing companies who pay more than non-profit making organizations still comes to only about one week's wages of a junior research assistant). ASLIB is, in fact, Government subsidized through the Department of Scientific and Industrial Research (D.S.I.R.).

Its members include, in addition to the industrial and commercial firms already alluded to, such organizations as Universities, technical institutions, Learned Societies, and public libraries. There are also private members. It could well happen that if a public library could not provide certain requested technical information from its own resources it could enlist (if it were a subscribing member) the aid of ASLIB, so that one might, at second remove, be helped by ASLIB. In general, however, its services are naturally restricted to its own members and many of its sources of information, if not always completely closed to non-members, are at least, difficult for the outsider to locate and to gain entry into.

Some of ASLIB's services which chiefly concern us here are—

(*a*) *Information Service*. It is presumed that members do not regard ASLIB as an ordinary information bureau for dealing with simple questions that can be answered from standard reference books. Nor can the lazy or incompetent technical writer expect ASLIB (and this applies to all other library services as well) to do most of the work for him. It can put valuable "tools" in his hands but he has to use them himself. In the case of ASLIB the information is often located in published reports and periodicals and the inquirer is then referred to these. In addition to the great number of books, journals and reports it takes into its own library, ASLIB is particularly expert in locating wanted material in other libraries and will usually succeed in arranging for it to be borrowed or photo-copied.

(b) *Index to Unpublished Translations*. ASLIB members have the advantage of being able to borrow or purchase copies of a great number of *unpublished* translations of technical and scientific articles (and therefore unavailable to the general public) translated into English. Over 200 organizations in various parts of the British Commonwealth contribute to the Index which, to date, records more than 30,000 items. I have before me as I write, a current list of translations made by the A.E.I.

ASLIB Publications

Member organizations receive free of extra charge the monthly *Aslib Proceedings* which, besides carrying general news of ASLIB activities contains the text of the more important papers presented at ASLIB meetings and also a list of the more important titles on library and information work taken from over 300 of the world's journals on the subject. Members also receive the *Aslib Book List* . . . a monthly annotated list of selected scientific and technical books in the English language. Every entry carries the recommendation of a subject specialist.

Members again receive, quarterly, the *Journal of Documentation* (devoted to the recording, organization and dissemination of knowledge).

ASLIB publishes various books and pamphlets which are available to members at special prices. The most famous of such publications is the *Aslib Directory*. It lists practically every library in the country . . . not only the National and Public Libraries but those of seats of learning, professional and trade organizations, industrial firms and research organizations and so on, and gives useful details about each: the resources, facilities offered, times of opening, etc. Listing is done by subject (so that we can look up, for example, where to get information on Tobacco) and also by town. It is probably the best thing of its kind yet done but is not intended to supply the answer to every question. For example, the latest edition available to me as I write, contains no reference to the International Christian Police Association, presumably because this worthy organization, whilst having, in its offices, a number of reference books, has no real specialist library in the sense that ASLIB understands it.

Moreover, if we were pursuing that perennial topic—the effect of smoking on health, and made application to a tobacco firm's research library, it is hardly likely that the information would be impartial. We would have to seek additional information elsewhere. Thus, because a subject is mentioned in the *Aslib Directory* it doesn't necessarily mean that our search is at an end.

The Aslib Directory (which you may be able to see in some larger public libraries) is useful also in showing the extent of inter-library co-operation.

Some other ASLIB publications are—*Index to Theses Accepted for Higher Degrees; Handbook of Special Librarianship and Information Work* and *British Scientific and Technical Books.*

ASLIB has a fine library and most of the books are available for members to borrow.

There are various other services. ASLIB (3 Belgrave Square, London, S.W.1) will send further details.

In this present chapter, as throughout the whole book, the aim has been to give as much succinct information as possible without going to the extreme of wearying the reader with elaborate detail. Such specialist books as Holmstrom's **Records and Research in Engineering and Industrial Science** are naturally useful for those who want to go into more detail.

In November 1962, the National Lending Library for Science and Technology was opened in the buildings of a sixty-acre wartime shell-filling factory at Boston Spa, Yorks. The initial stock was 350,000 volumes and 12,000* periodicals, drawn from 109 countries. The intake is calculated at over ten million words a day. It is not surprising to learn that the size of the library will be doubled within a decade.

In officially opening the Library, Lord Hailsham (then Minister for Science) said that human knowledge was growing at a most rapid rate and the need for documentation, classification and bibliography was most evident.

* Currently approximately 18,000.

CHAPTER XII

LITERARY REFERENCES

GUIDES to Literature seem to be as prolific as the Literature itself, but a book that has earned for itself a well-deserved reputation as a standard work of reference is **The Oxford Companion To English Literature.**

Since its original appearance, it has been reprinted several times with additions and corrections and the latest edition should, of course, be referred to when seeking more recent allusions.

For a review of literature in all its branches—albeit from a U.S.A. angle—**The Bookman's Manual,** by Bessie Graham, is admirable for the purpose. Authors of all countries are alphabetically listed under classified headings, such as *Fiction, Essays, Drama*, etc. There are also large sections dealing with reference books, annuals, etc. All the books of each author, or in each category of reference books are listed in chronological order, with publisher and (U.S.A.) prices.

The following can be useful: Magnus, **Dictionary of European Literature, Cambridge History of American Literature.**

Book "Outlines"

It is often necessary to know, in a nutshell, what a book is about, without having to read or re-read it. There are several (chiefly children's) books, such as **Tales from Shakespeare,** but an example of book outlines useful to the research worker is **Outlines of Great Books,** edited by the late Sir J. A. Hammerton. (Amalgamated Press, Ltd.)

This is described as "comprising two hundred and fifty of the World's Most Famous Works of History, Philosophy, Science, Religion, Poetry, Biography, Travel, and Criticism, Outlined in their Author's Own Words. With a Portrait Gallery of the Authors."

It stems from an earlier Amalgamated Press part-work, the five-volume **World's Great Books,** long out of print but normally obtainable through antiquarian booksellers (or to be seen in some libraries) and, I find, quite useful.

Two useful books giving well-written outlines of fiction books are Keller, Helen Rex, **The Reader's Digest of Books** (Macmillan Co., New York), and Baker, Ernest A., and Packman, James, **Guide to the Best Fiction, English and American, including Translations from**

Foreign Languages (1932). See also Nield, J., **A Guide to the Best Historical Novels and Tales.**

See also Baker's **Guide to Historical Fiction.**

Another U.S.A. publication is **Masterpieces of World Literature in Digest Form.** (Ed: Frank N. Magill) . . . "a dictionary of famous plots." Some 500 books, old and new, are covered (by no means too sketchily), each plot "digest" being preceded by a critique and a list of characters.

Another U.S.A. book is—

Outlines of Shakespeare's Plays (Watt, Holzknecht and Ross).

This gives an annotated *Dramatis Personae* of each play and then an act-by-act synopsis of the plot. It is prefaced by sections on Shakespeare's life; his theatre; the sequence of his plays: his sources; and some suggestions on reading Shakespeare. There is an index of characters and places mentioned in the plays.

The following (by no means exhausting the list) are also useful—

Bennet, J. O'D., **Much-Loved Books.**

Cartmell, Van H. (Ed.), **Plot Outlines of 100 Famous Plays.**

Goodman, R. A. (Ed.), **Plot Outlines of 100 Famous Novels.**

World-Famous Books in Outline (Odham's Press).

For *Characters in Fiction see* Chapter X (Biography).

Fiction

Likely to be much used in British libraries is Cotton and Glencross' **Cumulated Fiction Index.***

Book Reviews

Mention might be made here of the *Book Review Digest* (U.S.A.) which digests and indexes book reviews taken from over seventy-five leading American and British journals (excluding academic ones). It gives physical details of the books reviewed and, by a system of simple coding, indicates (approximately) what each reviewer thought of the book.

When reading through literary journals (if they are one's own property) one might well cut out those reviews which particularly interest one, and treat them as Press Cuttings for filing.

Quotations, Proverbs, etc.

It is feared that many writers use these books to convey the impression that they are well read and have quoted apt remarks extempore.

---

* *See also* Andrew Block's bibliography: **The English Novel**, a cross-index covering practically every novel and every novelist between 1740 and 1850.

A far better way of using them is to make the selected examples a nucleus about which we can build up our own ideas. There are many such collections. The old ones are not necessarily out-dated, but most people will prefer one which includes selections from modern authors. Reference should be made to more than one book, because, apart from the difference in actual selections given, and subjects treated, different dictionaries are complied on different plans. For example some have a bias towards the familiar: others, the less hackneyed. Some emphasize modern authors. Some have a bias in favour of U.S.A. writers . . . and so on. Most, however, are classified by author, and then by themes.

When an old established book of quotations is modernized it may be found that some of the lesser-regarded entries are cut out to make way for the new. If you cannot track down a quotation from modern editions, try looking through the old.

Typical standard works are—

Adams, F. P., **F.P.A. Book of Quotations** (emphasis on modern authors).

Bartlett, J. A., **Familiar Quotations.**

Benham, W. Gurney, **New Book of Quotations.**

Flesch, R., **The Book of Unusual Quotations.**

Stevenson, Burton, **Book of Quotations,** a fine, big book.

Hoyt's New Cyclopedia of Practical Quotations.

Dictionary of Quotations and Proverbs. Everyman Library. "This dictionary represents the work of many successive compilers, English and U.S., and the authors it quotes, known and anonymous, are legion. Traditional sayings and modern currency are both incorporated."

The Oxford Dictionary of Proverbs is well known, and international in scope is H. Davidoff (Ed.), **A World Treasury of Proverbs.**

A book of a different sort, old, but still very useful, is Bent, S. A., **Short Sayings of Great Men** (1882).

Here, the various sayings are grouped together under the subjects' names, together with biographical notes of the person, and details of the circumstances under which the saying was uttered. Thus we can ascertain when, where, and why Pope Gregory made his classical pun about "*Non Angli sed angeli*," and whether Oliver Cromwell made any remarks worth perpetuating. The book is prefaced by a list of authors, whilst there is an index of sayings, so that the book works both ways.

Anthologies also come in this class. If we wish for several quotations on Dogs, Fishing, or London, we might first look up bibliographies to see what anthologies there are on the subjects. Most of the books of quotations just mentioned contain "classic" sayings. For the lighter side, there are scores of books such as—

Herbert V. Prochnow, **The Speaker's Treasury of Stories for all Occasions.**

Jacob M. Braude, **Handbook of Humour for all Occasions.**

An old book still of value to preachers etc., is—

Scott and Stile's, **Cyclopedia of Illustrations for Public Speakers.**

There are also dictionaries and concordances of the works of various authors such as Shakespeare, Shelley, Jane Austen, Burns, Dickens, Thomas Hardy, etc. Cruden's **Complete Concordance** in various editions, full or condensed, is a handmaiden to the study of the Bible. Other standard books of reference on the Bible are Peake's **Commentary** and Hastings's **Dictionary,** to name but two of very many.

The "Syntopicon"

Mention might conveniently be made here of the **Encyclopædia Britannica's** publication, the **Syntopicon** (i.e. a "pointer"). It consists basically of a set of 54 volumes; standard "Great Books" of the Western world covering Science, History, Philosophy, Mathematics, Theology, Poetry and some fiction. Seventy-four authors spanning thirty centuries are represented, though why, for example, Herman Melville is there whilst far better novelists are not, is difficult to say. The books are not in any way summarized, condensed or "digested." The key to the whole collection is found in two volumes entitled "The Great Ideas." These contain 102 chapters each one dealing with such a great idea as Angels, Aristocracy, Desire, Evil, Evolution, Good, Liberty, Love, Man, Truth, Tyranny, and Wisdom. Though complete in themselves, these essays but summarize the matter. Each idea treated has references to the subject-matter contained in the set of books. There are, in all, some 163,000 such references. Thus, whereas the usual quotation books give us, all too often, a ragged selection of oddments, we can, in the **Syntopicon** read, if we feel like it, all that many of the great minds of the past have had to say on, for example *War*. A useful aid to the philosophic type of research worker.

Poetry

We often wish to trace a poem of which we remember only the first line or the title. Or we may wish to find poems written, on say, Hens, Holly, or Hospitals. Help will be forthcoming from such books as—

Granger's Index to Poetry (with Supplements).

The Oxford Dictionary of Quotations.

Essays: General Literature

Certain volumes consist of essays or speeches (usually over a range of subjects). Essays often deal with whimsical, intangible things that do not warrant devoting a whole book to. To trace individual essays, etc., in such books we can consult the *Essay and General Literature Index* (U.S.A.).

Essay and General Literature Index Volumes from 1900, edited by Minnie E. Sears and Marian Shaw, is an index to about 40,000 essays and articles in 2,144 volumes of collections of essays and miscellaneous works. This is a "dictionary" index, and includes all author entries, subject entries, and title entries which have been considered necessary. The material under an author's name is arranged—

1. Author's works.
2. Works about the author.
3. Criticism of an individual work by the author.

This book deals only with books published since 1900, but essays, etc., *written* before 1900 are included if the collection anthology or the like in which they appear (or re-appear) was *published* after 1900.

The original work covers the period 1900–1933 but supplementary volumes have appeared. These are now issued semi-annually and are cumulated in one-, three- and seven-yearly periods.

It is a useful work despite the fact (for British research workers) that it is a U.S.A. work. Much of the material can, however, be obtained in English libraries.

"Curious" Books

There are many books wherein the authors have, with incredible industry, collected thousands of curious facts for the diversion and amazement of a gaping world. Such books are worth noting, as they may contain facts needed to fill up gaps in one's inquiry. Examples of these are—

The Guinness Book of Records—possibly the best modern book of its kind available today. It deals with the largest the smallest, the leastest and the mostest, etc. As the facts (e.g. sports records) are constantly changing, the book is periodically revised.

Bombaugh, C. C., **Facts and Fancies for the Curious** (1905) "—from the Harvest Fields of Literature."

(*See* also earlier works of a similar nature by **this** author.)

Brewer, E. C., **Dictionary of Phrase and Fable.**

Brewer, E. C., **Reader's Handbook.**

(And several more books of this nature by the same writer.)

Every bookman should be acquainted with **Brewer's Phrase and Fable,** first issued over eighty years ago. In it we can look up—among other things—the origin and meaning of phrases such as "Dead Sea Fruit," "Medea's Kettle," find out why Martello Towers are so named; who was "Soapy Sam," etc. The older editions contain a concise bibliography of English literature, alphabetically arranged under authors.

The latest edition of **Phrase and Fable** has been completely revised and re-set.

The **Reader's Handbook** gives "famous names in fiction, allusions, references, proverbs, plots, stories and poems," an English and U.S. bibliography, an original list of authors, and dates of dramas and operas. It is also by Brewer.

On similar lines to Brewer is **The Reader's Encyclopedia** (Ed. Benét, W. R.)

Chambers's Book of Days is accurately described as "A miscellany of popular antiquities in connexion with the calendar, including anecdote, biography, and history; curiosities of literature, and oddities of human life and character."

Hone's Every Day Book (1838).

Wright, **Century Book of Facts.**

Walsh, W. S., **Curiosities of Popular Customs.**

Walsh, W. S., **A Handy Book of Curious Information.**

Walsh, W. S., **A Handy Book of Literary Curiosities.**

Walsh, W. S., **Heroes and Heroines of Fiction.**

Ripley, R. L., **Believe It or Not.**

Gerwig, Crowell, **Handbook for Readers and Writers.**

Timbs, John, **A Popular Dictionary of Facts and Knowledge.**

Timbs, John, **A Million of Facts.**

Timbs, John, **Things Not Generally Known,** and other such works. (Timbs wrote about 150 volumes.)

D'Israeli, Isaac, **Curiosities of Literature,** a classic of its type. Here we have entries such as "Literary Forgeries," "Political Forgeries and Fictions," "Introducers of Exotic Flowers," "Pamphlets," "Literary Impostures," etc.

There are also books of the "Inquire Within" type, such as **Pearson's Reference Book.** An Amalgamated Press publication, **Everybody's Inquire Within,** is full of "curious" information, well illustrated and containing many *modern* topics not found in older works.

Notes and Queries

This is a weekly paper which inserts literary, historical, and antiquarian (but not scientific) queries, free of charge, but confines them to those which cannot be answered from the usual reference books. Replies are expected to embody some research. They are unpaid, but one suspects the writers get a thrill of pride at the evidence of their superior knowledge when it is printed. Before inserting the query, one should look up the indexes of back numbers to ascertain whether the query has already been dealt with. Should the query not have been dealt with before, one should be prepared to wait some time before the letter is printed and the information (if any) trickles through. If this medium is used, it is as well to lay one's plans well in advance.

The indexes of *Notes and Queries* are worth searching for out-of-the-way information. They cover the entire run of the journal from 1849. Several counties issue their own *Notes and Queries*, such as the Devonshire and Cornwall *Notes and Queries*, running without a break since 1900. The existence of these can usually be traced from county bibliographies.

There is a French counterpart to *Notes and Queries* and also a U.S. *Notes and Queries* (from 1941).

Many of the old magazines ran a "Notes and Queries" page. Old volumes of *The Gentleman's Magazine* type of periodical yield interesting facts, especially in the realm of bibliography and obituary, to those who are willing to search.

Three useful volumes of extracts from *The Gentleman's Magazine*, *1731–80*, have been published: **Dialects, Proverbs and Word Lore; English Traditional Lore;** and **Manners and Customs.**

A general Index to 27 volumes of *The London Magazine* (1732–58) was published in 1760. Many large libraries have a "run" of such volumes and, as already indicated, they can be a gold-mine of interesting facts.

"Letters to the Editor"

There are few journals which do not carry this valuable feature. An interesting psychological study could be made as to why people write to editors. Very often it is for the free publicity which can thus be obtained for worthy causes, or a public pulpit for those who have something worth saying (or something which certain editors think will start a mild literary dog-fight, and so cause rival camps to rush to buy the paper to see how things fare). Then there are people who divulge curious and apparently irrelevant information such as that they went to school with a companion who had fourteen Christian names. There are the "Is this a record?" folk. Many people simply love to see their letters and names in print, and delight to find that they have provoked a discussion. Replies come from unexpected quarters—from people who know amazingly out-of-the-way things, and who would probably never have divulged them otherwise.

When the inquiry is an important one, make sure that you have followed *all* the correspondence from its conception up to "this matter is now closed." One correspondent may well make an allegation that is soon shattered by another correspondent.

The garnering of this information is dealt with in the coming chapter on Press Cuttings, but the researcher, instead of gathering any general information from this quarter, may like to pose a question on a particular topic, and await replies. The paper to which the query is submitted should receive careful consideration. Some papers are very "low-brow," others the reverse. Some prefer only erudite matters. Others are "popular." Some letters are, in effect, authoritative but unpaid articles on learned matters from important people. Unless your problem is of interest to others, it will not be accepted for publication. The shorter, and the more to the point it is, the better.

Never be afraid to state that you are writing a book on the matter. Few days go by without requests such as the following appearing in certain papers.

> I am collecting material for writing the biography of Watts E. Dunne, the eighteenth-century eccentric. I should be grateful if anyone having any hitherto unpublished papers, letters, etc., bearing on the matter would kindly let me peruse the same . . . etc.

This often brings invitations to visit private libraries, and also letters from utter strangers, crammed with useful information.

You also get this sort of thing—

> I have been informed that Dedleigh Drigh the poet once wrote an ode to a Cement Mixer. I cannot find this in any collection of this writer's works. Can anyone inform me where it may be found? It begins like this . . .

If you are lucky, you will have people from Boston, Billericay, Barnes, and Bournemouth rushing to inform you.

Translations

The ability to read, at least, one foreign language is a great asset to the properly-equipped research worker. It is true, as we will soon see, that a good deal of foreign material has been translated into English, but plenty remains untranslated and, in many cases delay in translating leads to loss of topicality.

When the Belgians left the Congo a writer, striking whilst the iron was hot, came out with a book on the political issues involved. One newspaper critic suggested that the author was rather at sea when dealing with public notices and proclamations, etc., that had been issued by the Belgians (in French).

To write a really original biography of, say, Johann Strauss and not pick over other men's "meat," we would have to go to many German-language sources.

At one time translation usually meant the Classics (or famous foreign novels) in translation. Now there is a deluge of technical material to deal with. French we usually take for granted in educated people. German is very useful for technical work and Russian is coming to the fore. For work on old documents Latin is essential.

A fantastic number of Technical, Scientific, Economic, etc., reports as well as general news items are published daily all over the world, and a vast army of translators is at work on what are deemed the most relevant. Electronic aid is now enlisted.

Much has been heard of "machine" (electronic) translating. As I understand it at the time of writing (and the situation is bound to improve) a "fine" and "literary" translation is not expected. It is sufficient to get the gist of the matter so that it can be classified and filed. *Then*, if necessary, a more "finished" translation can be made by a human translator.

The Times has published a booklet: **Freeing the Mind** containing a series of articles, on mechanical handling of language and information which had previously appeared in the *Literary Supplement*.

As mentioned in Chapter XI, before engaging in any translating from foreign periodicals, it is most prudent to discover whether the material has already been translated. If we are ASLIB members we have a great advantage here. See also such sources as—D.S.I.R. *Translated Contents Lists of Russian Periodicals*; *Translations Monthly*, lists translations, from all languages, currently deposited at the Special Libraries Association Translation Centre, Chicago.

If we want to find out whether **Three Men In a Boat** has been translated into, say, Russian, the place to look for this information is the U.N.E.S.C.O. *International Index of Translations*.

Here, with acknowledgement, is an abstract of a typical technical translation as announced by the Office of Technical Services, U.S. Dept. of Commerce. The name of the journal concerned is given, with particulars on how and where to order a copy of the translation.

> This article is a denunciation of the pharmaceutical monopoly in Venezuela. Because deficiency diseases are prevalent, and prices must be kept within reason, State Control of the pharmaceutical industry is considered to be a necessity.

CHAPTER XIII

MSS. SOURCES—PUBLIC RECORDS—GENEALOGY

RECORDED information need not necessarily be printed in book form. There is any amount of information recorded in handwriting—material which was never intended for public use—such as private diaries, letters, etc. Furthermore, there is MS. material written before the invention of the printing press.

MSS. Sources

Many private diaries, letters, etc., are in private hands, and whether we can use them or not is a personal matter, depending on our relations with the owners. If, for example, we are writing the biography of a certain person now dead, we can announce the fact in the "Letters to the Editor" columns of certain literary Sunday newspapers, and appeal to owners of any interesting, unpublished material relating thereto to let us know. If our work is approved, we will be granted access to much useful material.

Ancient deeds, charters, and other MSS. attract the attention of some research workers. Not all such documents are "dry as dust." Behind the crabbed, antique handwriting is the work of some human soul who lived centuries ago.* Many museums and public libraries keep old parchment deeds, etc., relating to the district.

See Jenkinson, H., **A Manual of Archive Administration,** also **A Repertory of British Archives,** compiled for the Royal Historical Society by Hubert Hall, assisted by Research Students of the University of London, 1920.

There is a special MSS. Department of the British Museum, where dozens of students are always to be found, poring over MSS. Our national repository is—

The Public Record Office (Holborn, London)

This contains national records dating from the time of the Norman Conquest, brought together from many sources. Here, increasing use is being made of the National Register of Archives which was started in 1945 under the Historical Manuscripts Commission. The work of the Commission includes the collection and collation of

---

* Dr. A. L. Rowse's **Raleigh and the Throckmortons** was based on a hitherto unknown Elizabethan diary and brought fresh facts to light.

details of ancient and modern documents in private hands and with local authorities, churches, hospitals, schools, banks and companies.

I should mention that centuries-old Rates Books and the like discovered in say, the Town Hall, are often turned over to the local public library.

The City of London Records Office (Guildhall)

This is regarded as being the finest and most complete repository of ancient municipal archives in existence. There are charters, statutes, administrative rolls and books from 1252 to the present day; records of the Old Bailey, Guildhall sessions from 1603, financial records from the sixteenth century, together with a wealth of other historical documents.

There is also, of course, the Scottish Record Office.

Provincial museums, libraries and religious bodies also often possess fine collections of documents. Ask your librarian if he knows of such local collections.

Genealogical Research

In a book of this size, it is not possible to go into details of specialized research. Exception must be made, however, in the case of genealogical research, since this is a subject which interests a great many persons.

Some are merely curious as to who their ancestors were; some are frankly snobs, and would like to claim Norman blood. Others, more practical, are interested in their descent so that they can claim an inheritance. Many engage in this research as a hobby. Others put the matter into the hands of the Genealogical Society, who have a great Index of over two million slips, giving details of baptisms, marriages, burials, wills, etc., culled from old parish registers, leases, indentures, and the like.

The work is difficult, and often made increasingly so by the lack of co-ordination of those who possess old records. Some antiquarian societies have collected local records and published them. (See, for example—the *Parish Register Society* publications.) If the records are quite lost, we cannot cry over spilt milk, but a legitimate source of complaint is that many records are left to moulder, say, in some damp nook behind the organ in a village church, and can be seen only at some inconvenient time, and for an exorbitant fee.

Most standard works on the subject of genealogy give lists of published compilations of old records. Many of the books on genealogy are old, and obviously do not include the published results of more recent parish, etc., record researches. But records of the last half-century or so are not difficult to look up. A useful work is Rye, W., **Records and Record Searching, a Guide to the Genealogist and Topographer,** second edition, 1897.

This shows how to compile a pedigree, or the history of a parish; how to locate obscure documents published by little-known societies; how to examine parish registers, State papers, ecclesiastical and monastic records, manorial records, cemetery books, and printed collections of wills.

Typical helpful books are—

Marshall, G. W., **The Genealogist's Guide.** This should be supplemented with the more modern Whitmore, J. B., **A Genealogical Guide.**

The Library of Congress, **English and American Genealogies,** (1910) lists books and papers dealing with many families—a useful aid in tracing ancestry.

Select Biography of English Genealogy, Harrison H.

Gatfield, **Guide to Books and MSS. Relative to English and Foreign Heraldry and Genealogy.**

Browning, **Americans of Royal Descent.**

Burke, **Family Records.**

Budger, **Index to Printed Pedigrees.**

Thomson, **Catalogue of British Family Histories,** and the indexes to **The Genealogist, Ancestor** and **American Genealogist.**

In "popular" style and useful is Pine, Leslie, **Trace Your Ancestors,** also John Unett, **Making a Pedigree.**

Historians will find much of interest in the numerous volumes published by H.M.S.O. of Calendars of Patent Rolls, Close Rolls, State Papers and Letters, Domestic, Colonial and Foreign, preserved in the Public Record Office. See Galbraith, **Introduction to the Use of Public Records.**

An invaluable work for the historian and topographer is **An Index to the Charters and Rolls in the Department of Manuscripts, British Museum.**

At the General Register Office (England and Wales) at Somerset House, London, one may, for a small fee, examine wills, etc.

There are such works as—

British Record Society **Index of Wills Proved** and now preserved in the principal Probate Registry.

But, as already hinted, though there are several useful indexes, these are often of a very specialized nature and interest is chiefly confined to certain branches of the legal profession.

To the *Punch* references on p. 8, we can add one on ancestor-tracing that appeared in the 9th Aug., 1961 issue.

CHAPTER XIV

TOPOGRAPHY AND TRAVEL: LOCAL HISTORY

MAPS are handmaidens to practically every form of study—geography, history, economics, etc. We can follow a travel book much more easily if it has a map, or if we have an atlas. We can appreciate literature the more if we can see on a map exactly whereabouts are the places described.

Maps, Gazetteers, etc.

The chief producer of maps in this country is a Government department, The Ordnance Survey.

The maps are of a very high standard, and issued in all scales. The usual scale for appraising the country in a fair amount of detail is the 1 inch to the mile. Larger scales, $2\frac{1}{2}$ inches, 6 inches and 25 inches to the mile are issued, the latter used by estate agents and property owners.

On the other hand there are smaller scales, 4 miles to the inch being a popular one with motorists. The O.S. issue a catalogue which should be applied for by those interested.

Apart from general maps, there are geological maps, etc., and also maps (with a booklet of description) of Roman England, Medieval England, civil air maps, Admiralty pilots' guides, etc. The British Museum has one of the finest collections of maps in the world.

See also the work of the Geographical Section of the General Staff.

Atlases

There are scores of these, of greatly varying size, completeness, price, quality, usefulness, etc. All general encyclopedias have an atlas section, or have maps incorporated with the text. Special atlases have been issued dealing with Biblical history, military campaigns, colonial growth, etc. Many atlases reveal unexpected supplements, such as details of flags, coins, the planetary system, etc. An atlas is practically indispensable to the proper understanding of such subjects as history. We can even get a modern atlas of maps of the moon.

The new *Times* atlas is excellent, whilst many cartographers produce useful and varied atlases suitable for all types of study. Philip's **Readers' Reference Atlas of the World** is a magnificent publication.

The **Europa Motoring Guide to Europe** has maps and gives tourist information on the whole of Europe.

The maps and tourist information given in the A.A. and the R.A.C. guides and the publications of petrol, etc., companies are often useful.

Mention might here be made of **National Geographic Magazine Cumulative Index, 1899**—(American).

Royal Geographical Society, *Library Catalogue*, also *General Index to Journal*.

Gazetteers

These are really indexes to maps, and often give, in a very small nutshell, an account of the population, products, etc., of a town or place. Their chief use is in locating a place. Further details we can read up elsewhere. Naturally only the more important places are mentioned in the general gazetteers. A small village in, say, Sussex would be overlooked. In such a case, if we know the county, or rough location, we can consult a guide-book dealing with the district.

A standard gazetteer is **Bartholomew's Survey Gazetteer of the British Isles.**

For research into current affairs it is most important to consult an up-to-date atlas, as, in this turbulent world, place names are continually changing and new ones come along. When doing research in local history, however, the old maps and county guides, etc., are often very informative.

Guide Books: Home and Abroad

One publisher or the other usually has a county-by-county series of guide books going. (And likewise with foreign travel guides.) As always, in research work, the latest editions should be consulted for the latest information but some of the older books such as the famous **Highways and Byways** series have a nostalgic interest and the older **Baedeker's Handbooks** are far more useful than their publication dates suggest. (There are, of course, up-to-date editions.) There are also those guide books of Fodor and of Nagel and, also, of English and of U.S.A. publishers. We usually consult those appertaining to foreign countries but foreign publishers also issue guides to Great Britain and it is often salutary to see ourselves as others apparently see us.

Tourist Information

In these days when holidays abroad are so popular, tourist-agency brochures and other sponsored travel booklets proliferate exceedingly. Although much is just "sales talk," many of the booklets, especially those issued by the tourist boards of various governments, contain useful and (usually) brightly-written information about a certain country's geography, history, social customs, gastronomy, and the like, and are worth collecting and keeping. The information in railway, etc., maps in some of these booklets is often difficult to find elsewhere.

Most public library reading rooms now maintain (in season) a large collection of sea-side town guides and other brochures.

Regional and Local Topography

Practically every public library has a "local" collection though, in a few cases this may be just a musty bookcase full of scholarly tomes bequeathed by a departed savant. I hope you will, when the need arises, find the places where the public librarian is keen on local history and—subject to the staff and time available—indexes much of the local newspaper(s) and additionally makes a press-cuttings collection of local interest. In addition to the **Subject Index to Periodicals** (*see* Chapter XV) the Library Association regularly issues a series of **Regional Lists** (by counties or groups of counties) wherein we may find references to periodical and newspaper articles dealing with, say, Hertfordshire.

Many counties are blessed with county magazines, as for example, the *Sussex County Magazine*, and the *Herts Countryside*. The editors of these do not want the usual "guide book stuff" from contributors and so one can usually find, in such magazines, some out-of-the-way information.

See also the **Handbook of County Bibliography.**

Some counties have a Record Office and an official Archivist.

Another source of topographical information, often overlooked, is *Kelly's County Directories*, whilst we must not forget *Railway Guides* (**ABC** and, formerly, **Bradshaw**). These give, apart from fares and times of trains, useful information regarding distances, population, market and early closing days, etc. Coach time-tables and Air Line guides are also useful.

Local History

A very useful modern book is **Teach Yourself Local History** (Francis Celoria). This indicates, clearly, various sources of information and is much recommended.

See also Hoskins, W. G., **Local History in England.** A stimulating book that lets some fresh air in on what can be a "stuffy" subject.

The various County Archaeological Societies publish voluminous *Transactions*.

Parish Registers

These are mentioned, briefly, here since they are often consulted when one is looking into Local History.

These unique records were instituted on 5th September, 1538, by Thomas Cromwell, the Vicar-General, who commanded that, from that date, the clergyman of every parish must enter in a book details of all local marriages, baptisms, and burials. A few parishes kept registers before Cromwell's order, the earliest record extant being that of Tipton, Staffs (1513). Not recent, but still useful books to read on this subject are Dr. Cox's **Parish Registers of England** and his **How to Write the History of a Parish.**

Besterman in his **Bibliography of Bibliographies** lists some parish registers.

See also the publications of the Parish Register Society, and **Local Records, Their Nature and Care** (Redstone, L. J., and Steer, F. W.).

Archaeological, etc., Papers

There is an immense number of these.

A useful series of annual lists is Gomme, G. L. (later volumes edited by others). **Index to Archaeological Papers, 1891–1914.** These extend back to 1665.

The work is carried on in the Library Association's *Subject Index to Periodical Publications** (*see* Chapter XV). This Index is rather good at listing the publications of local Field, etc., Societies.

As with research into other subjects, information often comes from previously unplumbed sources. For example, in **The Norwich Subscription Books** (A Study of the Subscription Books of the Diocese of Norwich 1637–1800) the author, E. H. Carter has been able to discover and analyse valuable new facts from entries concerning the licences granted to the clergy, schoolmasters, doctors and midwives. People in these professions had, to ensure ethical standards of conduct, to "subscribe" to the Thirty-Nine Articles, the fundamentals of the Established Church. Hence the title of the book.

The BBC's publication, **The Historian At Work** is an excellent general guide and has a useful bibliography.

* Now the *British Humanities Index.*

CHAPTER XV

PERIODICAL PUBLICATIONS: CURRENT AFFAIRS

THE number of periodical publications in this country alone is overwhelming. It is safe to say that there is no trade, profession, shade of opinion, etc., which has not at least one journal to cover it. (Science publications are discussed in Chapter XI.) Some publications, such as four-page leaflets describing the common round of a country parish church, appear to be of so little importance to the world in general that we tend to ignore them.

But let no one say that a certain newspaper or periodical is too insignificant to be worth filing. Boys' magazines going back for half a century or more before, say, 1939, were, by many contemporary parents, thought utmost trash and were often banned from the house. Nowadays some quite erudite research is going on regarding Buffalo Bill, Sexton Blake, Nelson Lee, the boys of Greyfriars School . . . and other colourful characters who featured in these lively and much maligned weeklies.

Other periodicals, important in their restricted spheres appear to be too obscure to be worth the trouble of locating. Others, however, have important circulations, reflect contemporary opinion and methods, and contain items of information a long time before they appear in book form.

Those fact-finders who seek "popular" items of information should not easily be put off by the apparent exclusiveness of some journals. *The Financial Times* for example, may seem, to the layman, of interest only to those who aspire to be "something in the City." I have found the statistics it publishes of great use in obtaining up-to-date assessments on such subjects as how much the country spends on (say) weddings per annum.

Until comparatively recently, research among periodicals has presented difficulties not only with regard to indexing (a matter soon to be discussed) but also *physical* difficulties. Files of old periodicals are bulky to store and expensive to bind. Their pages get brittle and easily torn. Now, thanks to micro-filming (and apparatus for re-reading the tiny print) the problem is well on its way to being solved. There is, in fact a *Union List of Newspapers on Microfilm in American Libraries* and one firm, Microfilms Inc., issues a list of foreign periodicals available in this medium.

Some useful books containing lists of periodical publications (a complete list for the British Isles and including the principal overseas and foreign journals) are—

Willing's Press Guide (annually with quarterly supplements). First published 1874. This contains a list of about 7,000 names, giving details of the publication day, price, address of publisher, etc., in alphabetical order. A very valuable feature is an Index to Class Papers, where we can discover, for example, the periodicals dealing with Bee Keeping, Church of Scotland, Dentistry, Fish Trade, Waste Trades, Zoology, etc. Another list shows the periodicals published from various towns.

Mitchell's Newspaper Press Directory is on similar lines.

The Writers' and Artists' Year Book. Few free-lance journalists are without this. It lists the principal English, Commonwealth and U.S.A. journals in alphabetical order, but makes no claim to being a complete list. Only journals offering any scope for the professional writer are listed, so that the smaller fry of papers, or those which do not accept outside material, are omitted. Unlike Willing's book, it gives a very clear idea of the type of contents one may expect to find in each paper. There is a classified index of papers and magazines, but this is not so detailed as *Willing's Guide*. The point is that Willing's caters more for newsagents and advertisers. The **Writers' and Artists' Year Book** contains lists of publishers, press-cutting and photograph agencies, etc. See also the Library Association's **Guide to Current British Periodicals** (ed. M. Toase). This also gives details of such things as readership level, type of advertisements, length and number of book reviews, regular features and indexes.

Corresponding to Willing's and to Mitchell's directories in this country, are those of Ayer and of Ulrich for U.S.A. periodicals.

A study of these Press directories will therefore show that there is a multitude of periodicals on every possible subject, each issue being full of information. Some of it may be very dull, stodgy and "correct." Some may be "popular" and of doubtful accuracy. Some may be propagandist, and otherwise coloured or distorted. But, anyway, it is all grist for the mill of the researcher. A rich field—though at times a troublesome one—to be used generally when the information cannot be found in handier books.

Older Newspaper Writing

Periodicals are especially important in ascertaining contemporary opinion or eye witness reports of now historic events.

Collections of such reports are occasionally published as, for example—**Eye Witness** (John Fisher) which is an anthology of

British newspaper-writing, beginning with the description (from *The Times* of 11th August, 1815) of Napoleon's departure for St. Helena.

Some fine pieces of writing—essays and the like—have first appeared in the pages of periodicals. In many cases commercially astute individual authors or, in other cases, editors, have gathered such writings and have re-issued them in book form. But this is not invariably so. Sometimes it is left for a compiler of anthologies to dig out almost-forgotten articles from dusty files. At random we may quote such a collection as **Contributions To the Edinburgh Review.** (*See* the C.B.E.L. for some others.) These compilations are very useful and time-saving if we wish to read only *typical* pieces.

In this chapter we will first seek, as far as practicable, an answer to the following questions—

1. What were the forerunners of such modern Press directories as those of Mitchell, Willing, Ayer, and Ulrich?
2. What indexes are available to these older publications?
3. What indexes are available to modern periodical publications? (*a*) English, (*b*) U.S.A. and foreign.
4. Where can available files of (*a*) English periodicals, and (*b*) English newspapers be seen?
5. Though we may expect to find many foreign periodicals listed with English in library catalogues, where can specifically (*a*) U.S.A., (*b*) Foreign, journals *be seen*?

1. Older Periodicals

The **Cambridge Bibliography of English Literature** can be helpful here. See also: **Tercentenary Handlist of English and Welsh Newspapers, Magazines and Reviews,** *The Times*, 1920, and Crane, R. S., and Kaye, F. B., **A Census of British Newspapers and Periodicals** (1620–1800), useful for ascertaining what periodicals were published at a given period.

2. Indexes to Older Periodicals

Without an index, the finding of any particular article in a pile of periodicals is worse than looking for a needle in a haystack. Unfortunately, until fairly recent times, indexing periodicals has been done only sporadically. Now a good deal of work is being done in this direction. Inadequate indexing is being improved and more anonymous articles identified.

Let us examine some available indexes in their chronological order. From 1802, we have Poole, W. F., **Index to Periodical Literature** (1802–1907).

Though now discontinued, this is such a valuable reference tool that it has been re-issued in modern times (reproduced by photo-offset). It spans a period of 105 years and covers 479 titles. See notes in Winchell regarding its intelligent use. One deficiency in Poole is remedied by a latter-day **Poole's Index Date and Volume Key.** An abridged edition covering 37 periodicals (1815–99) with Supplement to cover 1900–04 was published in 1905.

This was followed by **The Annual Library Index** (1905–10), which in turn was taken over by **The Reader's Guide to Periodical Literature,** published by the H. W. Wilson Co. (*see* following notes under 3*b*). See also the **Annual Magazine Subject Index** (1908–52), and **Nineteenth Century Readers' Guide to Periodical Literature.** (Wilson, N.Y.). As I write, I note that the Wellesley College Library, Mass., U.S.A., is preparing an **Index to Victorian Journals** (1824–1900).

All the above are U.S.A. works.

The finding of such a work as **Review of Reviews Index to the Periodicals 1890–1902** may prompt the research worker in the older-periodicals field to make further inquiries whether other, similar, indexes exist. There is also Cotgreave, Alfred, **A Contents-Subject Index to General and Periodical Literature, 1900.** This is one of the best guides to earlier magazines such as *All the Year Round*.

3. (*a*) Indexes to Modern English Periodicals and Newspapers

A most useful and almost indispensable "tool" when dealing with English journals is the Library Association's **British Humanities Index*** published annually since 1915 (with a break from 1923–5) and quarterly (with an annual cumulation) from 1954.

It is the work of voluntary contributors, and currently covers about 400 British journals (past volumes covered, also, some U.S.A. and foreign journals)—by no means all "academic" or "heavy"—whose contents are thought to be authoritative and reliable, yet acceptable to the general reader. Ephemeral and trashy articles do not therefore jostle carefully written articles by experts. Journals covered by the regular engineering and science, etc., abstracting services (*see* Chapter XI) are not normally included, neither is fiction or verse. From 1961 the volumes carry an author index.

There is also a **Subject Index to Welsh Periodicals.**

One of the very few English newspapers which has ever been indexed (or whose index has been made public—since all newspapers index their contents for private information and records) is *The Times*, which has been regarded as the nearest approach to an

* Formerly the *Subject Index to Periodicals*.

"official" newspaper we have. An official index to *The Times* began in 1906, and is in progress, being issued at present, bi-monthly. It is very full, containing references to date, page, and column. Not quite so detailed, but useful, especially for the period before 1906, is **Palmer's Index to "The Times,"** also issued quarterly, from 1791.

See also **Index to "Glasgow Herald"** (from 1907), useful also as a guide to *dates* of reports in such other newspapers as *The Scotsman*. Different newspapers record the same important event at much the same time.

If you are a regular subscriber to a journal it is usually (but by no means invariably) easy to find out whether an index is published since an announcement is normally made to this effect. The **Reader's Digest** issues an excellent annual index . . . free to those who apply. I have, myself, the volumes for the past thirty years and thanks to the indexes, I can readily find information over a wide range of popular topics. But few subscribers seem to be aware of these indexes as, so far as I can see, the publishers are very coy in announcing the fact.

Whilst some journals do not issue annual indexes, many have a contents page or column. These may be cut out and pasted in a cuttings-book for convenient reference. Indeed many of the abstracting and technical information services reproduce, facsimile, the contents pages of various journals.

The only way to compensate for the lack of indexes in some popular journals (which may have no contents-list) is to take press-cuttings (a subject dealt with in the next chapter).

3. (b) Indexes to U.S.A. Periodicals and Newspapers

The Reader's Guide to Periodical Literature (previously mentioned in passing) is issued as a semi-monthly list, with frequent cumulations and a biennial volume. It lists, alphabetically by subject and by author, articles (though not, normally those academic and technological ones best covered by the regular abstracting services) published in U.S.A. journals only.

There is an *Abridged Readers' Guide* but this is not much value to English libraries.

The Dramatic Index contains a record of the stage in the U.S.A. and England as shown by the periodical press of the past decades. It is an index to all dramatic articles and illustrations, a record of production and of who's who on the stage. There is a portrait index to actors, actresses and playwrights, and a list of dramatic books and plays of the year.

See also the following publications of the H. W. Wilson Co.—
Agricultural Index.
Education Index.*
International Index to Periodicals devoted chiefly to the Humanities
and Science.

4. Finding the Files

(a) ENGLISH PERIODICALS. On a national scale there is the **British
Union-Catalogue of Periodicals** (of the World, from the seventeenth
century) contained in some 440 British libraries. This has some
140,000 titles. This is continued as the **British Union-Catalogue of
Current Periodicals,** which includes all periodicals new since c. 1950
as well as material additional to that already published. On a
regional scale there is the **London Union-Catalogue of Periodicals.**

The British Museum Library has a wonderful collection of periodicals and newspapers both at Bloomsbury and Colindale. As a minimum, most libraries file *The Times* and the local newspaper. The
bigger the library, the more periodicals are filed. Some of the periodicals in the library are filed for periods ranging from six months to
seven years or more, and some sold after use (*see* Press Cuttings,
next chapter). The larger libraries bind up all the journals. The
Patent Office Library has a splendid collection of scientific and technical magazines. The research worker is thus able to see many journals
whose circulation is, normally, strictly restricted to the Trades concerned. The issues for the last year or so are kept loosely in box files
on reference shelves. They are then tied in bundles and kept in reserve
until the binders can deal with them. Then they are sent to their
final positions on the upper floors. There is an extensive card index
to periodical publications, which gives the location of various volumes.

One can purchase (with supplements) a catalogue of **Periodical
Publications in the Patent Office Library.**

It will be appreciated however that it is not only out of the question, by reason of cost, for individual libraries to take in every issue
of every magazine published, but it is also, as regards storage space,
impossible to find room to keep all the back numbers for lengthy
periods. Thanks, however, to the co-operation between libraries,
each co-operating library in a certain area (as, for example, the
London Region since 1953) undertakes to take in and to store,
certain journals so that between them they have extensive files of a
wide range of periodicals, particulars of which are given in a regional
Union Catalogue. Thus, if you wish to see an article in, say, *Family
Doctor* for June, 1958, your local public librarian can find out which

* A British Education Index is published by the Library Association.

public library in his Region holds the files (and for what period) and he will make arrangements for you to see the actual file or to have a photo-copy made.

London Medical Schools pool their professional periodicals, and so do some other corporate bodies such as the Herts. Special Libraries Group and the Coventry Information Group. See the *Aslib Directory* for further details.

(*b*) ENGLISH NEWSPAPERS. The precise dividing line between a periodical publication and a newspaper is one which bothers many librarians.

If we are using the British Museum Library (which takes in some 8,700 current British periodicals and some 3,000 foreign ones, besides having files of those now defunct), we shall find that newspapers dating from 1800 are now housed at Colindale, near Hendon, Middlesex—a good way from Bloomsbury. Periodicals issued by learned societies and other organizations are entered under the names of the issuing bodies, not under "Periodical Publications." The entries for periodicals are found by looking for a cross-reference under the title, as there is now no index to the "Periodical Publications" volumes. It should be made clear that these are part of the main Catalogue, and are quite distinct from the Catalogue of Newspapers.

The entries for newspapers (which include a large number of foreign ones) appear under the name of the town from which they were first issued. The *Irish Times*, for example, would appear under *Dublin*. To ascertain what town the periodicals originally came from, consult the index volumes.

If one has much research to do among newspapers and periodicals it may be best to apply to the British Museum Library. It should be noted, however, that, although the most important journals are bound as soon as possible, it must be some weeks before a file is made up, and unbound newspapers cannot be consulted unless one can show that the matter is very important.

Many leading newspapers make a regular practice of letting research workers study the files, and a small fee is often asked, depending on how far back one wants to look, and sometimes on the time spent on research. The files for the last few months are generally available free and obtainable without formality. For the older files it is as well to notify the librarian in advance so that the heavy file can be brought up from the store rooms.

The smaller journals usually have no formal regulations for consulting their files, but, if the files cannot be seen in any library, a letter should be addressed to the secretary of the journal concerned. Usually, one is given all facilities for genuine research.

5. Periodicals and Newspapers in Foreign Libraries

(a) U.S.A. For U.S.A. periodicals in the leading libraries of the U.S.A. there is a Union Catalogue. It can be assumed that files of most of the leading foreign periodicals are available somewhere in England's libraries but it may so happen that in specialized research we may wish to consult, say, the files of a U.S.A. magazine kept only (according to the Union Catalogue just mentioned) in one Middle West University library. Provided one is prepared to be patient and not averse to some financial outlay, the prospect is not so forlorn as it would have been a few decades ago, thanks to photo-copying services. Perhaps one of the U.S.A. commercial information bureaux might act on your behalf.

U.S.A. Newspaper Indexes. One of the most useful is the **Index to the New York Times** (from 1913). The index entries are so full that they form, in fact, synopses, and will often answer an inquiry without reference to the newspaper itself.

(b) FOREIGN. Some foreign Governments maintain public reading rooms either at their embassy or legation offices or at some convenient centre. At such places, the leading periodicals of the country can usually be seen.

Current Affairs

For those whose work necessitates constant reference to current affairs, such as those studying politics, etc., **Keesing's Contemporary Archives** is indispensable. Many public libraries take it. It is a kind of diary of current affairs, the news of the day being summarized and sent in weekly bulletins to subscribers who file it in a special binder. Cumulative indexes are a valuable feature of this work. A U.S.A. publication on similar lines is **Facts On File,** consisting of a weekly *News Digest* (of current world affairs) with a fortnightly cumulative index.

Deadline Data (on Foreign Affairs) is a U.S.A. production on a card-index system: 3,000 cards are initially supplied, with weekly supplements.

The Annual Register has been published annually since 1758, and reviews events at home and abroad, political, commercial, literary, dramatic, legal, etc.

A paperback edition of this valuable work, re-entitled **World Affairs,** is now published by Penguin Books.

Annual reference books such as **Whitaker's Almanack,** the **Daily Mail Year Book** and **Pears' Cyclopedia** review events of the past year.

Hazell's Almanac was once a rival to Whitaker, but is no longer issued. One can bear it in mind, however, when looking up events of past years (1886–1922).

See also Hansard (Chapter IX). Pronouncements in Parliament frequently make front-page news.

Useful for the student of Affairs are (among others)—

The International Year Book and Statesman's Who's Who.

The Statesman's Year Book.

The United States in World Affairs (O.U.P. for Council on Foreign Relations).

Survey of International Affairs and also **Documents on International Affairs** (published for Royal Institute of International Affairs), also the latest edition of—

Desmond Crowley's **The Background of Current Affairs**

Britain—an Official Handbook. (Central Office of Information.)

The Europa Encyclopedia (loose leaf: bi-monthly) and **Orbis** (for non-European countries) provide, as Europa Service, a survey and directory of political, economic, cultural, journalistic, constitutional and religious organizations throughout the world.

Public Affairs Information Service is a non-profit association of (U.S.A.) libraries, and its purpose is to publish a weekly Bulletin, listing by subject, current books, pamphlets, periodical articles, Government documents and any other useful material in the field of economics and public affairs.

Most countries issue their Year Books. A random glance at a well-stocked library shelf devoted to such matters reveals **Swedish Year Book, Indian Year Book and Who's Who, Chinese Year Book** (in English), **Anglo-American Year Book, Handbook of Uganda,** etc.

CHAPTER XVI

PRESS CUTTINGS

CURRENT periodicals are so cheap and plentiful that there is no point in making notes from them. It is quicker and better to snip out the relevant paragraph or article, and file if for future reference. It is really surprising how the information accumulates, and the majority of working journalists, especially the free-lances, owe their success to an extensive cuttings-file (plus, of course, the knowledge of how to use it).

There are several press-cutting agencies which cover any chosen subject very thoroughly, and charge so much per hundred cuttings. The addresses of these agencies can be ascertained from such a literary year book as Black's **Writers' and Artists' Year Book.** They are particularly valuable if you want *all* the news about something or somebody (all the reviews of your last book, for example). It is obvious that it is scarcely possible for the average person to look through every periodical published in England (and important foreign ones) *every* day. This can be done only by a large organization with a trained staff.

Again, one pays only for the cuttings one receives, and if one's subject is not mentioned in the papers for several weeks, one does not have to pay for unrequired copies. This means that it is sometimes cheaper to subscribe to an agency, since the cost of the papers one buys (often in vain) will come to more than the cost of the agency fee.

But this applies only when it is essential that one has all the available press notices relating to one subject. As a general rule, one is interested in a few subjects in a general way, and it is then far cheaper to make one's own press cuttings. But whether the cuttings are supplied by an agency or by oneself, they must be filed properly. A drawer full of miscellaneous cuttings is not much use. A great many people make cuttings, and stuff them casually into wallets, etc., affirming that they will wait until they can afford a cabinet or cuttings-book to store them, and then make a nice job of it. The result is that before they can get a suitable cabinet, they have such a jumble of unsorted cuttings that the task of classifying them seems so formidable that the project is abandoned.

It is almost as bad to start off with a big cabinet and the idea of filling it up as quickly as one can. By all means add to it, but ask, of every cutting, "Are you necessary?" It is not the *bulk* of the file or cuttings-book that matters, but what *information* it contains. Of course, you will not shirk the task of filing really valuable information. This takes time, and a certain evening each week should be devoted to the task, otherwise a huge pile of papers will accumulate. This routine work may well be attempted when the brain is tired with creative work.

It is not a bad idea, to keep cuttings for a week before filing. Some "cool off" so to speak.

Before you snip your first cutting make up your mind what subjects you are going to cover. The wider your field, the less thoroughly you will be able to cover it. Specialization pays. Even the simplest topic can be split into dozens of sub-headings and aspects, as will shortly be demonstrated.

Further, it hardly pays (at least, for the professional) laboriously to file current news items (which can easily be looked up in one of the commercial news-indexing services described in the section "Current Affairs") nor science items which can be obtained, as abstracts, already printed on cards for filing. (*See* Chapter XI.)

Again, decide what system of filing you are going to use. You will have all your allotted time devoted to filing new cuttings, and little time to waste re-arranging cuttings which might better have been sorted out years ago. Naturally, as one goes on, one discovers better ways of filing, cross-indexing, etc., but a general system should be established.

It might be mentioned here that if you file your cuttings regularly you constantly see the various headings marked on the envelopes and so have your collection well under review.

As a general rule, there is little to recommend the rigid cuttings-book. For one thing, it is bulky. It requires an index. It is cluttered with cuttings not now required—cuttings which have been superseded by others covering the ground better. The cuttings-book is superior to the envelope-file only where the subject is highly specialized (or of narrow scope), or where the cuttings are of permanent value. Thus, if we were collecting cuttings relating solely to our local sports club, we could paste them in a book, and compile an index. At the most, a mere dozen or so cuttings a week would have to be treated—possibly fewer. Moreover, it would be easier to consult the cuttings in a book. Their value would improve with age.

Many journals publish regular notes on Nature, Health, Gardening Hints, "How-to-Make" articles, etc., and invite you to cut them out. These are of permanent interest as a rule, and when pasted neatly in a book, form, in effect, a new book on Gardening, Cookery, Keep Fit, or whatever the subject is.

For the bulk of cuttings accumulated for general journalistic purposes, however, the only workable plan is the envelope-file.

For many years the writer used 6 in. × 9 in. envelopes cut in half, and arranged in cardboard boot-boxes. Some workers prefer larger envelopes stored in vertical files. These are an advantage in some ways, especially as one does not have to fold up the cuttings. But small cuttings are liable to get lost in large envelopes and most of us have not, at first, the necessary file. The boot-box file can be started by anyone, and, when funds permit, a wooden cabinet invested in.

The most obvious way of cutting the newspaper to pieces is to use scissors, and this is perhaps the most convenient way when, for example, cutting up *The Times* on a crowded desk, but it is far quicker and neater if one has "clear decks" to lay a thick piece of millboard under the sheet and make four slick cuts with a penknife or one of those knives which take razor blades. On the back of the cutting mark the date and the name of the paper from which it was taken.

For the sake of demonstration, suppose you are interested in four subjects—Dogs, Child Welfare, South Africa, Whaling.

You will start off with four envelopes marked with these titles, and in them place all the cuttings relating to the subjects. (If you have to fold the cutting, fold it with the title side *outwards*. One instinctively does the reverse.) After a while, the envelopes will be getting very bulky. It is time to subdivide further. Let us look at the "doggy" cuttings. We could sort them into envelopes bearing the new titles—

DOGS: VARIOUS BREEDS.
DOGS: HEALTH.
DOGS: AMUSING TALES OF.
DOGS: FAMOUS, IN LITERATURE.

The Whaling cuttings might be subdivided—

WHALING: NORWEGIAN.
WHALING: EXTINCTION OF WHALES.
WHALING: WORLD TRADE.
WHALING: BY-PRODUCTS.

So we will go on until *these* envelopes are fairly full. Let us look through the first one, "DOGS, VARIOUS BREEDS." We could probably subdivided this into—

DOGS: Terriers.
DOGS: Alsatians.
DOGS: Mongrels, etc.

And when the "Terriers" envelope becomes full we can further subdivide it, so that in course of time, when we have thousands of cuttings, we can soon pick out an envelope relating, say, to mongrels that have become "film stars." We shall not have to turn out a bulging envelope simply labelled "Dogs" and spend an hour in sorting its contents in the vague hope that we *may* have a cutting relating to the matter. We could not have provided all these subdivisions at first, as for one thing we could not possibly know exactly what we would need, and if we could, the collection of empty envelopes would be confusing and depressing.

Take yourself sternly in hand regarding any envelopes marked MISCELLANEOUS. It is so very easy to relegate, here, any cutting whose classification is not immediately obvious. You can "save" a lot of time this way and then regret it later.

The envelopes themselves must be arranged in convenient groups, and this is easily done by inserting tabbed markets of thick cardboard. One might even keep a special drawer for "Dog" matters, and have markers inscribed "BREEDS," "HEALTH," etc.

The BREEDS envelopes should, if at all numerous, be arranged in alphabetical order—AIREDALES, BOXERS, COLLIES, etc.

A snag which one soon meets is when a cutting refers to two or more subjects and one does not know which envelope to place it in. Taking our four examples again, we might have a cutting relating to Child Welfare in South Africa, or Children and Dogs. The writer's plan is to cut up slips of cardboard, about the size of visiting cards, and write on one, say, "SOUTH AFRICA, *see* Child Welfare in Other Countries." This slip is then placed in an envelope marked "SOUTH AFRICA, Various References to," whilst the cutting itself is placed in "CHILD WELFARE, in Other Countries."

Often a cutting requires more than one cross-reference. Quite frequently we find a cutting which summarizes the contents of several we already have. These can therefore be scrapped. Again, it is often possible to write the whole import of several cuttings in a dozen or so words on a slip of paper. Whilst constantly adding to the file, be constantly weeding out too. Several cuttings which relate to each other might be found in one envelope, but are not sufficiently numerous to warrant a fresh envelope. These should be pinned together.

Although the running of a Press-cuttings file *does* take time and effort, it is generally a good investment, for we not only have a great deal of interesting and out-of-the-way information not found in the usual reference books, but this information is conveniently brought together. I have just taken, absolutely at random, an envelope from my files. It is marked BARBERS and endorsed "*see also* HAIR," so I get out this envelope too. Over a hundred cuttings are before me, some gathered thirty years ago; some last week. I am in full admiration of, and would certainly use, the bibliographies which professional librarians may have made concerning tonsorial art, but I doubt whether all their references would contain *all* of the information in my cuttings file. Certainly the "odd" pieces of information would leaven the "encyclopedia stuff" if I chose to write a "popular" article on the subject . . . the reason I ever started collecting cuttings about barbers.

There are occasions when you have a number of Press cuttings relating to a certain subject but wish you had more . . . quickly. Suppose you have been collecting cuttings from "general" newspapers and magazines relating to, say, the odd and sometimes (it seems) farcical things for which a Fire Brigade is called out. I refer to such things as rescuing unappreciative cats from trees, recapturing pet monkeys from rooftops and bringing up starving dogs from old mine shafts: freeing small boys' large heads from iron railings, coaxing would-be suicides from dizzy heights . . . and so on. Anything, in fact, except putting out fires. If you look through files of the fireman's journal (**Fire**) you will find, most likely, reports of other such capers . . . often with salty comment. See *Punch*, 15th February, 1961, for an article on these lines. The work of the author (E. S. Turner) is well worth studying as many of his articles (and his books) plainly show (to perceptive tyro fact-finders) the research work behind them. To be as effective as Mr. Turner, one needs his light touch, of course, in the presentation of the facts.

You could, in theory, think up the idea first and then go to the files of **Fire** for information. In actual practice one is usually struck, in casual reading by the oddity of a reported happening and then one decides to keep an eye open for others. Usually one has such a lot of these dossiers building up that one can afford to bide one's time. But the subject might suddenly become topical and there is then the need of extra information, quickly.

The foregoing description of collecting press cuttings is that of a system which the writer has used successfully over a number of years. There are, however, other systems which their users claim are equally effective, and which may be briefly described here.

Instead of putting all cuttings relating to one subject in one envelope, some prefer to number them as they come, irrespective of their subject. Thus cutting No. 467 may relate to the resignation of the local mayor, No. 468 may refer to a riot in Bombay, whilst cutting No. 469 might be about some amazingly active nonagenarian.

These cuttings are made up into packets, each containing, nominally, fifty items. If some cuttings are very bulky, however, less than fifty may go in one bundle. The idea is to get all the packets the same size. Some put the bundles of cuttings in an envelope, whilst others clamp them between two pieces of card, held by rubber bands. These packets are also numbered. Thus the cutting about the Bombay riot, mentioned above, might be in packet No. 9 and would be referred to as 9/468.

An index is now compiled, listing all the *subjects*, just like an encyclopedia. Naturally we have only to enter the same subject once. For example, when we get any more references to Bombay riots we just add their numbers to the index—which should preferably be of the card variety. Our index might look like this—

BOMBAY. Riots in, 1/35 3/137 6/269 10/468.

Cross-references can be made quite easily, whilst a note can be taken of the date when any envelope was made up. Most journalists in full stride collect about fifty cuttings a week, so it is a simple matter to write out a list from which we can see when packet No. 17 was made up, or what packets "cover" 1961.

The time taken in making the index is compensated for by the time saved in packing the cuttings into plain fifties, and not sorting them out into the various subjects. There are many disadvantages, however. It is not unlikely that, in order to deal with our inquiry, we have to get, say, twelve cuttings from twelve different packets. There is a risk that the cuttings will get mixed up and not be put away again in the right packets, or in the right order.

Some writers start off by taking twenty-six files, one for each letter of the alphabet, and in each of them inserting some leaves of stout paper, each marked with the subject to be treated. Thus the A file might contain sheets marked ACTORS, ALHAMBRA, APPARITIONS, etc., whilst the B sheets would be marked BALLADS, BILLIARDS, BOXING, etc. When we get cuttings on these subjects, we paste, them *lightly* to their respective sheets, so that if it is necessary to remove the cuttings (for rearrangement or replacement) it is a simple matter to tear them away. Subdivision of the main subject is easily effected by adding additional sheets to follow the main one. As the file is loose-leaf, this is quickly done. Thus we may eventually have sheets marked ACTORS, MODERN BRITISH; ACTORS, MONEY EARNED BY GREAT; ACTORS, HOBBIES OF; ACTORS, VIEWS ON AUTOGRAPH HUNTERS. The advantage is that the cuttings are carefully classified, and kept flat, thus making reference easier. On the other hand, extra work is involved in pasting and repasting as classification proceeds.

Books have been made with pages resembling large envelopes wherein cuttings may be stored. These are obviously quite unsuited for permanent collections (if only on the score of their cost), but they are very useful for holding temporary batches of cuttings, especially when the cuttings are kept only until one's article is written and then destroyed.

As previously mentioned, the writer's preference is to devote each drawer of his filing cabinet to a special subject, such as HOBBIES, ENGLISH COUNTIES, BUILDING AND ARCHITECTURE, etc. Some writers prefer to arrange their envelopes in strict alphabetical order, so that PAPER, PARLIAMENT, PIANOFORTE, RAILWAYS, SELDEN SOCIETY, TOLSTOY, and WAR MEMORIALS, might follow each other. Between the envelopes themselves, cards of the same size might be inserted, bearing cross-references. Thus our file might contain an envelope marked LIBRARIES, followed by two cards marked, respectively, LOUVRE, Museum of, *see* PARIS and LYON KING-OF-ARMS, *see* HERALDRY; then an envelope marked MAGNETISM, and so on throughout the alphabet. The drawers of the filing cabinet will simply be marked A–E, F–H, etc.

The writer will have to use his own wits to decide which is the main issue in cases where a cutting refers to two distinct subjects, both of which are already represented in the files. Thus I have before me a cutting relating to what is said to be the smallest inn in England, near Dorchester. I ask myself, "If it is filed away, under what circumstances would I be likely to look for it again, and in what section of the files?" I might be writing an article on old inns, and would naturally look in my envelope marked OLD INNS. On the other hand, I might be writing an article on the Dorchester district, and wish to pick out some topographical "curiosities." In this case I would look in the DORSET envelope. Therefore both envelopes have, apparently, equal claims on this particular cutting. Strictly speaking it does not really matter which envelope has the cutting, provided a ticket, bearing the cross-reference, is inserted as already described. As a matter of technique, however, it is well to adopt a logical method of deciding which is the major topic.

I think I should put the cutting in the INNS envelope. If I intended to write an article on the topographical curiosities of Dorsetshire, I would look up the INNS, TOLLGATES, PREHISTORIC ANTIQUITIES, FOLLY TOWERS, OLD COTTAGES, and similar envelopes. If, however, I intended to write an article on inns, it would hardly be logical to search all through my ENGLISH COUNTIES drawer, which has nearly a hundred envelopes. I might spend hours on it. Instead, I open the DORSET envelope and find a note to the effect "*See* Inns,

Tollgates, War Memorials, and Folly Towers." I thus know that I
have a cutting relating to inns. I also know that I have no cuttings
relating to the prehistoric antiquities or old cottages, and so I am
saved the trouble of looking in these envelopes.

Hints on cross-references can be gleaned from good catalogues,
such as those of the British Museum Reading Room (Subject Indexes).
See also in this present book Alternative References in Index (next
chapter).

No two research workers will proceed on identical lines. Some
very business-like research workers will probably relieve the burden
of cross-referencing by the use of punched-card filing systems, such
as the Copeland-Chatterton cards, for information of a specialized
kind (described in the next chapter).

CHAPTER XVII

USING THE BOOKS: NOTE-TAKING

HAVING found a certain number of books dealing with our subject, our task has only just begun. All this bibliographical searching was just a preliminary. We must learn how to use the books.

Get into the habit of never using a book more than once in the same inquiry, eschewing this sort of fidgetiness. In view of what follows on "Speed in Reading" one might suggest here that you set yourself a time limit for studying each book.

Many books of the "How to Study" type have been published, and a well-established work is Sir John Adams's **The Students' Guide** (revised by Rodney Bennett).

Taking Notes

It is a vexed question among research workers how far notes should be taken. Some maintain that the memory should be relied upon more. A writer known to the present author would, when he had to write an article on a certain subject not well known to him, retire to a library, and read up the subject from several sources. He made no notes, except, perhaps for a few dates, figures and spelling of foreign names. He then returned to his study and wrote the article from what he had remembered. Only the outstanding events were recalled, and these were the points that mattered.

This is all very well if one has a good memory, and can write up the article soon afterwards. A great many research workers, however, gather thousands of facts before they make serious attempts to classify them and write their article or book. Notes are therefore a necessity. What is written, remains. The memory may fail one. Moreover, it is easy to arrange into various divisions facts written on small pieces of paper. It is not so easy to marshal one's thoughts when the brain may be teeming with other irrelevant things.

The professional author who intends writing up his notes for publication should be very much on his guard, especially when working from *one* book, against copying the original author's own words (unless a direct and acknowledged quotation is sought). It is only too easy at a later stage to forget which are your own words and which are another author's. A *little* unintentional duplication of phrasing may pass muster but if it is in the least overdone, one may be accused of infringing another's copyright.

Since note-taking is hard work, the ideal is to jot down as much information in as few words as possible. At the same time, ultra brevity is to be avoided, as otherwise when one comes to examine the notes one may find an abbreviation which seemed very ingenious and time-saving at the moment, but whose meaning is now quite forgotten.

Use of Contractions and Abbreviations

There are various systems of "speed-writing" and abbreviated writing advertised in literary journals. A knowledge of shorthand is a valuable asset, on account of the ease with which notes can be taken, and the time spent in learning will be amply repaid. However, longhand, with various contractions, suffices for many. The reader can, if need be, invent a few simple abbreviations for his own use. A well-known one is to refer to the main topic by its capital letter only. Thus if you are taking notes on Plumbago, you would write it in full the first time, and subsequently refer to "Exports of P." or "Chief P. producing countries." "The" can nearly always be omitted or written /. The present writer substitutes "g" for "ing" and would write "h. racg" for "horse racing." Such abbreviations as "tn" for "town", "ch" for "church," etc., are well known. Many concise encyclopedias give long lists of abbreviations. There are special abbreviations for different branches of research. Thus in genealogy, = means "married to," whilst *ob.* means "died."

The Essential Point

These short cuts, though they do save a little time, are comparatively unimportant. True economy is effected by a careful choice of what one does write. Remember, what you want is *the essential point*. What is more, you want this point in your own words; how it appeals to you; what reference it has to your inquiry.

The best thing to do, is to read through *a chapter* or *section* of a book and then write down, in your own words, a summary. Glance back to see that you have missed nothing of importance. Have you grasped the point? In any case, what are you reading the book for? When you are really *studying* a book you may well indulge in imaginary philosophical discussions with the author. In quick reference work you usually require *information* only.

As you come to read the notes afterwards, ask yourself "Are the facts correct?" "Up to date?" "Biased?" "Mere opinions?" "Only 'good enough'?" (*See* further in this chapter under Checking Facts.)

More Haste . . .

Notes should obviously be legible. All proper names should be written in BLOCK CAPITALS and particular care given to *figures*. *Ink* is far better than pencil. It allows finer, smaller writing, and a good fountain or ball-point pen requires little pressure. You may want to read your notes in ten years' time. For this reason, too, the notes should not be too abbreviated. Coherent English might take a little longer to write, but it saves time in the end. Get into the habit of making neat notes right away.

It is a good plan to make a full note of the name, author, date, publisher, etc., of any books used. It may be necessary to refer to them again, or they may be needed for a bibliography.

Cards or Notebook?

For note-taking, the present author prefers using cards, writing one item of information on each. Random thoughts can thus be written one after the other on the cards just as the inspiration strikes one. Afterwards the cards (measuring about $4\frac{1}{2} \times 3\frac{1}{2}$ in.) can be sorted out, and facts arranged in their order of importance. Only one side of the cards should be written on. When finished with, the writing can be crossed through with a blue pencil and the other side used. These cards are easier to handle than similar slips of paper or bound note-books.

At the top of each card, the subject of inquiry should be written. This is tedious to do by hand several hundred times, so use can be made of a printing set as used by children. A title such as SHELLEY BIOGRAPHY can easily be set up, and sub-titles such as Parentage, Education, etc., composed too, if you anticipate having several dozen such cards.

It is essential to have a cardboard box in which to file the cards, otherwise they will soon get into a chaotic condition and be of little value. A visit to a shop dealing in office requisites will settle this point. For other information about filing, see also in this present book under "Press Cuttings," and "Annotating Books."

If a notebook is used, let it be of the loose-leaf variety, and one in which the leaves are held firmly by press studs or springs, not by rings from which the perforated leaves soon break away. Write the main notes on the right-hand pages, leaving the left-hand side for extra notes and comments which crop up afterwards. Carry around a little pocket notebook to record various ideas and scraps of information one casually picks up.

Punched Cards

The punched card system is particularly useful for those methodical research workers who need very closely to analyse and "process" data. Precise details of the various systems such as the "Cope-Chat" can be obtained from suppliers of business-efficiency equipment. In general terms, the cards have holes punched just inside and alongside their four edges. Those holes on the upper and right-hand edges might be ready marked in alphabetical sequence, and those on the left-hand and bottom edges numbered from, say, 1–50.

Assuming (for the sake of an elementary example of use) that we are compiling data on how professional persons "retired" too early have successfully started a second career. We might, for coding, allocate a letter of the alphabet to various professions (say K for retired Generals) and a numerical code for types of employment or activity (say 14 for insurance work). Then, if one card carries information relating to a retired General who has been appointed to the Board of an Insurance Company, we take a hand punch and convert the holes K and 14 into slots. Later, if we wish to gather information, say, on "retired" people on Insurance Boards, we stack up the cards, ensuring that they are the right way round (by noting the position of a clipped-off upper right-hand corner or by similar means) and pass a knitting-needle through the No. 14 hole. On lifting the needle, those cards which have *not* had hole No. 14 (i.e. which do *not* relate to insurance) are impaled and carried up whilst those cards which *do* relate to insurance fall out by reason of the *slots* which have replaced holes No. 14. Alternatively we could, by passing the needle through holes K find, in a few seconds, all those cards relating to retired Generals. By first "skewering" at No. 14 position and then, form this selection, "skewering" at K, we could find all those cards relating to retired Generals on Insurance Boards.

The labour in punching the cards (in any case, usually done by clerical staff in commercial research organizations) is offset by the fact that the cards do not have to be filed in any special order. They can, of course, be cross-referenced (i.e. punched) in much more elaborate ways and sorted mechanically. The foregoing merely shows the basic principle.

"Fair Copying"

It frequently happens that one would like a complete copy of a magazine article to study at leisure instead of having to take hasty notes in a library. If the back number of the magazine is out of print it is a very simple matter now that "dry copying" machines are in wide use, for the Library, in which the magazine is seen, to run off a copy. The snag is that the magazine material is copyright. It is still occasionally necessary to write to the editor to ask for permission for a copy to be made (this is rarely refused to genuine research workers if the copy of the magazine concerned is out of print). Fortunately this time-consuming formality is not always needed nowadays since many publishers now subscribe to a "Fair Copying" agreement. Your librarian will be able to give you full particulars. In any case, you'll have to apply to him. In general terms, however, the co-operating publishers (of magazines, etc.), grant, without further formality, the right of a research worker to have one copy of the required material made, provided it is for *bona-fide* study and research purposes and not for sale as such.

Studying, Skipping and Skimming

Having obtained the books, the researcher might be appalled at the amount of matter he has to wade through. However, if we wish to find out something about Horsham, there is no need to read through a whole history and topography of Sussex. We just read that page or two which carries the information we want. In some works this is easily done by referring to an index. Other subjects do not lend themselves so easily to this.

There are three ways of dealing with a book, apart from reading it purely for distraction and entertainment.

(*a*) We may *study* it, reading it carefully and completely. At the end of every chapter or section, we may review what we have just read, making notes, weighing up the author's remarks and comparing them with those of other authors.

(*b*) We may *skim* over it quickly, missing whole pages (or even whole chapters), alighting on a paragraph here and there, to get a rough idea of its contents. Most readers do this when they receive a new book. By this means, we can see whether the book is likely to contain the matter we require and ascertain in what direction our study might lead us.

(*c*) Our search may not even necessitate looking at a single *chapter*, however rapidly. By means of the index we can locate those *passages* which concern us. It may be a fifty-word paragraph in a massive three-volume work.

Considerable experience is needed in skipping and skimming, but it is an art which the research worker will sooner or later acquire. It is discussed, in detail, later in this Chapter.

Use of the Index and Table of Contents

A good index is a great time-saver, but unfortunately many books have not an adequate index. Good indexes are models of industry. Several books have been written on the subject and there are specialists who engage in the work.

The least satisfactory of indexes are those which appear like this—

Belfast, 78, 86, 117, 174, 185, 198, 204.
Belfort, 35, 66, 307.

We may be looking for details of Belfast shipyards, and have to wade through all the references before we have exhausted our inquiry. Although we might strike lucky, and find references to the shipyards on page 78, how can we be sure that there are no further details on page 204? And—how are we to know that there are any references to shipyards at all? Of course, the entries may be cross-referenced, and on turning over a few pages we may find—

Shipyards, 117, 215, 219.

At first we cannot tell which, if any, refers to Belfast.

A far better type of index is one set out like this—

Belfast
Arms of the City	185
General description	78
High street	198
Linen industry	174
Protestant Cath.	204
Queen's University	86
Shipyards	117

The information is thus found at a glance, and we know what is, and what is not, in the book.

Another valuable form of index is that where the contents of each chapter are analysed, either at the beginning of the chapter or in the table of contents. Thus—

CHAPTER VII   Page 69
St. Bruno, 11th cent. saint—His birthplace at Cologne—Becomes high church dignitary—Decides to go into retirement with six others—The Bishop of Grenoble gives him valley of Chartreuse— He founds Carthusian order—His good works—His death.

Here is almost a "potted" biography of the man. An admirable arrangement, especially if coupled with a good index.

Another arrangement seen in some textbooks is to have a brief synopsis of each sub-section set in small type in the margin or inset into paragraphs. In many books, as here, the material is split up into convenient sections, each one clearly labelled for easy reference. Get to know of these short cuts.

Make sure you are looking at the *right* index. Sometimes there are two or more indexes: a list of place-names and a list of persons, etc. Where there are several volumes, the index is usually *at the end of the last volume*.

Alternative References in Index

This is a VERY important point to grasp, and one which will serve the research worker in good stead.

A good index *should* give alternative references but not all indexes are good.

Do not overlook the Latin and Greek forms of certain words: *Ceramics* for *Pottery*, *Petrology* for *Rock Structure*, *Ichthyography* for *Fishes*, and so on. But not all cross-references are couched in "classic" terms.

Suppose we are looking up in a reference book the properties of Oak and fail to find it. What else can we call oak? Try Timber, Wood, or perhaps Furniture.

Butterfly Collecting? Try Hobbies, Nature Study, Collections, Pastimes, etc.

It often pays to seek the key word of a multiple term. For example, in "Sulphur Sensitizers," the key word is normally *Sensitizers*.

The above are quite simple, but, as we have seen in the section on Catalogues, it can become complex.

Take for example a report of the Department of Scientific and Industrial Research. This is a Stationery Office report, and the S.O. is a Government Department—the Government of England. The report is probably catalogued under "England": subdivision "Dept. of Scientific and Industrial Research." Admittedly not easy for a novice to work out, but this line of reasoning will be developed after some months of acquaintance with library catalogues.

The Society of Arts is a learned society of London. Therefore its publications are listed under "London," subdivision "Learned Societies," further subdivisions, "Society of Arts."

Some listings, however, can prove tantalizing. An H.M.S.O. report on an inquiry into an explosion in a baker's oven was published on behalf of the Ministry of Transport and the Ministry of Aviation!

Most good indexes have certain cross-references indicated. For example—

Baden-Powell, Lord (*see* Boy Scouts)

Many research workers have failed to find what they want through not being imaginative enough to look up alternative entries in indexes.

A first glance at the table of contents and index should reveal several things: Who is the author? His status? The date of publication?

Does the contents list show the book likely to contain the information you require? You might already be acquainted with the matter treated. Is there a list of *Addenda* and *Corrigenda?* Are there any *Appendixes?*

Plan of the Book

A careful author gives considerable attention to the *plan* of his book. In fiction, this is not noticeable to any but those who make it their business to analyse literary works.

In a technical book, however, the plan is much more obvious. In the preface, the author generally calls attention to any special features of the book. The first chapter is usually a survey of the subject to be treated, and often contains just that bird's-eye view of the matter we want. Thereafter, each chapter should deal with a clear-cut division of the subject, working from simple to complex.

Series

A word on "series." Very often the word is applied to a collection of books covering a variety of topics, having little in common except their size, make-up, and binding, and usually, the price. Some so-called "series" are frankly a Miscellany, and often consist of cheap reprints of popular works. The uniformity of size and price makes them attractive and easy for the publisher to handle and sell, but these are not true "series" likely to be helpful to the researcher as such.

A true series should centre around a common theme such as Common Commodities, Modern Poets, Socialist Viewpoint, etc. The idea is that instead of having one huge volume covering the subject, the matter is divided up into specialized heads. Thus, instead of a work of encyclopedic proportions dealing with *all* common commodities, we have smaller books dealing with single subjects such as tin, flax, coal, etc. It follows, however, that, as these books are divisions of the same thing, they should be equal to each other. Consequently we should expect them to be alike in presentation, status of author, technical complexity, illustration, etc. If we find that a book on Gas Meters exactly suits our needs, we can feel sure that, if we later require a book on Laundry Chemistry, one in the same series is likely to meet our requirements again. One book would not be elementary, and the other highly technical. One would not have illustrations on every page and the other be quite unillustrated.

The above should be read in connexion with the notes on "Publishers' Catalogues" elsewhere. The whole point is that a research worker specializing, say, in Art, should know which publishers are likely to produce books of interest to him, and, in coming across a single volume of a series, be able to visualize the full scope of the series so that he can extend his inquiries in other directions, but on similar lines.

Date of Book

This, of course, is important to the research worker. A book without a date is annoying to reader and librarian, yet any number of books appear without dates. One is occasionally justified in thinking that this is not an oversight, but is usually done deliberately so that the publishers can palm off old books as new. Books bearing a date *a year ahead* of their real issue are not unknown!

There are certain reference books which bear the date of the latest printing (say, 1960), but which prove on investigation to have been last *revised* in 1945! Distrust the apparent newness of these books.

The real date of issue can sometimes be ascertained from important catalogues, either those in libraries or those sometimes issued by the big people of the second-hand book trade.

It will be appreciated that if a year book is dated (say), 1963, and on sale towards the end of 1962, the closing date for "copy" must have been in the early months of 1962.

Speed in Reading

It might be thought that speed in reading is an advantage. So it is, providing that one understands what one has read. It is hardly likely that any would-be research worker is a very slow reader—one who "speaks silently," i.e. repeats to himself, all the words he reads. The average rate of adult reading is around 250 words a minute, though a lot depends on whether the reading matter is "light" or "heavy." In some works, writers choose their words very carefully. Each word must be given its weight, and though the writing is not dull, it is less easily read than a light novel where we can skip many words at a time without losing the thread of the narrative.

Heaven knows, there are some frightfully dull works which the research worker must tackle in the course of investigations. Judicious "skipping" may lighten the task. Do not forget that some books are written especially for advanced students, so do not always think yourself dull if the writer is not always clear. His ideas may be on a

different plane to yours. If you persevere, you will eventually pene-
trate the veil, and really understand the book. The writings of other
authors may treat your author's difficult passages in a simpler way,
so that a difficult book is made easier by reading others dealing with
the same subject.

Habitual readers get into the habit of seeing two or three words
ahead. They read by sight and not by sound. Speed in reading is a
good thing provided it is not made at the expense of clear understanding of what is being read.

An excellent article, condensed from **The American Magazine,**
"Speed While You Read," by Robert M. Bear, Ph.D., appeared in
the **Reader's Digest.** In a nutshell, here are Dr. Bear's contentions.

We need to read a lot to keep pace with current affairs. Time is
limited, so—we must read faster. Most of us waste time in reading.
Do not "read silently." (Get a friend to watch your lips, or place
your fingers over your vocal chords to detect any vibration.) As an
exercise, force yourself to read, for five-minute intervals, a little
faster than is comfortable. Don't worry if, at first, you can't take it
all in. Keep a record of how many words you cover in each five-
minute test. Unless it is at least 875 (175 words a minute), almost
certainly you are a word-by-word reader.

Try to increase your span of vision. Train the eyes to sweep over
each line. Instead of reading from left to right of each line, glance
down the middle of each column. Try to take in at a glance the sense
of a paragraph. Practice skimming over your newspaper. Ask someone to describe to you the purport of a paragraph; then try to locate
that paragraph quickly. It is possible (in the manner of Theodore
Roosevelt and Thomas Carlyle) to skim at a glance the contents of a
page. Skimming-pace is from 800–1,000 words a minute. Normal
reading pace, according to this authority, should be 350–500 words
a minute.

Fortunately, Dr. Bear realizes that for analysis, criticism and enjoyment of style, reading pace may be as slow as sixty words a minute.

The present writer endorses the 1,000 words a minute *skimming.*
As a case in point, suppose we are writing a biography of Beethoven.
We wish to ascertain (*a*) when this great musician first became deaf,
and (*b*) was he medically treated for it? We have before us several
lengthy biographies, opened at a chapter dealing approximately with
that period in which we know Beethoven became afficted with deafness. (Though possibly we may have to "skim" earlier chapters to
make sure that our subject had no ear trouble in childhood.)

Now, our eyes glance rapidly over the pages, seeking certain *key
words,* e.g. *deafness, hearing, great misfortune, first signs of trouble,*

etc. As soon as we find such significant words we start reading
normally, backwards and forwards, from these "landmarks." Remember that, in literary research, we are reading, not for pleasure,
but, usually, to find a needle of reference in a haystack of a library.
Another book on this subject is **Quicker Reading,** by Harry Bayley,
designed particularly to help the hard-pressed business man get
through each morning's reading more quickly. This book can help
you to triple former reading speeds.*

Checking Facts

The research worker must learn to weigh alleged "facts." Authors,
being human, frequently put into print statements which are based
on misapprehension, faulty information, false logic, bias, bigotry,
unscrupulous propaganda, as well as slips of the pen or printing
mistakes. In a *Manchester Guardian* review of the H.M.S.O.
Documents on German Foreign Policy Mr. A. J. P. Taylor wrote—
"All State archives are stuffed with rubbish as every research-
worker knows; but there is little point in publishing them—except
to teach people not to believe all they read."
Usually, by working from several sources we find that one state-
ment cancels another. In any case, from the literary point of view
the essence of copyright is not in the factual matter in general, but
in the way facts have been selected and weighed up.
We are often advised to *get the facts right*, to *weigh up all the
facts*, and so on, before making a reasoned decision on some debat-
able subject. Less frequently heard, but no less important, is *get
the relevant facts*. Avoid piling up "fact" after "fact" until you can
make a selection only of those which fit in with a pre-conceived and
pre-arranged policy (unless you are a paid propagandist!). There are
several books of a "popular logic" type. One I have found very
useful (and amusing) is Jepson, R. W., **How To Think Clearly.**

Annotating Books

Readers are by no means agreed as to whether books should be annotated, except that library, or otherwise borrowed, books should
NEVER be marked. Some hold that a book becomes more personal if
notes and comments are written in it; others that annotation often
defeats its own ends. We may make notes on fly-leaf and margins
to our heart's content, but by the time we have so annotated dozens
of books, we should need a large index to our copious notes.
Personally, I use a kind of index. I take a book at random from

* Harvard University have sponsored "Reading Films" for public sale to teach
speed in reading.

my shelves. It turns out to be *Vagabond*, a collection of "open road" essays by J. B. Morton. I remember reading it at intervals on a walking tour, and, as particular paragraphs and thoughts appealed to me, I scribbled down their position on the flap of the dust jacket. Thus I see—

Hats, 79.	Inn Names, 85.
Soul of the Parks, 40.	Silence, 316.

There were about two dozen such references. They happen to be mostly abstract thoughts, but naturally they vary according to the type of book.

I therefore prepare some cards for my file index—one for each item. One would read thus—

INN NAMES. *See* "Vagabond." J. B. Morton.

In dealing with a book at a large library, I usually add its catalogue reference, so that I am saved the trouble of looking this up again should I have further occasion to use the book.

On this same card, I will write down all other references to Inn Signs I come across, all books on the subject I have, all photographs of inn signs I have in my files, and a star to denote that I have press cuttings as well. Thus when I come to write on Inn Signs, I have a wealth of information to go by.

All this takes time, but it is a sound investment. Possession of a well-indexed file and library is a valuable asset to a working writer. Some people keep a Journal or Commonplace book. Others record their thoughts directly in the index cards of their file.

Take the same subject—Inn Signs—again. I was passing an establishment called the "Star and Garter" just as a motorist was driving away. It occurred to me that the inn, in these modern motoring days, should be renamed the "Car and Starter." I scribbled this "gem" of wit in my notebook, and thence on the INN SIGNS card in the index. Later I was able to use it in an article. I should have forgotten it otherwise.

A useful book is—

Shawcross, Walter, B. A., **Elementary Précis Writing.**

Though the foregoing methods of dealing with notes and press cuttings may serve well enough for individuals . . . and they have certainly served, with profit, a professional journalist . . . more elaborate methods may be needed for industrial and commercial concerns; information bureaux; libraries, and the like, where full-time paid staff is available to do the work. This aspect is well covered in Vol. 2 (Filing, Indexing and Circulation) of Holstrom, J. E., **Facts Files and Action.**

CHAPTER XVIII

SOME OTHER SOURCES OF INFORMATION

A RESEARCH worker should never be so tactless as to expect professional men to answer professional questions except in the usual way of their business. Obvious examples are: solicitors, doctors, income-tax experts, consulting engineers, and the like. They have acquired knowledge by an expenditure of time and money which they hope to recoup with interest. In the same way, certain societies are formed and financed by kindred souls to protect and advance their own interests. They often possess valuable stores of information, which they naturally preserve for the benefit of their own members, who have paid for the privilege.

In many kinds of fact-finding it is sometimes necessary to engage an expert in his professional capacity.

I might mention at this point that *some* public libraries have contracts with experts who, for some reason (possibly out of gratitude for services the library renders or has rendered *them* will give an inquirer the benefit of their special knowledge. Such sources are, naturally, tapped (and always with great tact through the librarian) only when all other sources have failed.

On the other hand, there are societies formed to foster and publicize some object. It may be an attempt to establish bird sanctuaries, free dental clinics for Esquimaux; to encourage an interest in the works of some literary person; to reform some law or the other. There are thousands of these societies. Some are very active in their propaganda and maintain effective publicity departments. These welcome sensible inquiries.

Practically all the information gathered from such sources is naturally, partisan and, often, "commercial." There is nothing, however, to stop one from reading the propaganda put out by two or more rival factions. The news and views of, say, the anti-blood-sports organizations should be read in conjunction with those of the field-sports societies.

If one is devoted to a special interest, or if one is working for a business interest, it pays to belong to as many Societies and Organizations as possible, which look after your interests or, at least, to gather their reports and other publications. One who was keenly interested in preserving the amenities of the countryside would be in touch with such organizations as the Ramblers' Association; the

Commons and Footpaths Preservation Society; the Council for the Preservation of Rural England, the National Trust, and so on. From one Society one often hears of another whose aims are somewhat similar: a donation, for example, is often made by one Society to another as announced in their journals, etc., or Societies periodically group together to stand fast against something that concerns them all.

Apart from societies, as such, there are publicity bureaux maintained by the railway companies; steamship lines; Post Office; federations of electricity, gas, transport, etc., interests; Colonial and Dominion offices; similar offices acting for foreign countries, and countless other sources of information. The banks have information services for their clients. Many stores and newspapers run information bureaux.

Within recent years there has been a great increase in Public Relations Departments and Government Press Officers. News reporters, seeking "inside information" or "getting a line" usually resent the "flannel" caused by such officials, but the searcher after facts of a non-controversial nature will almost invariably find such P.R.O.s useful and helpful provided one gives them reasonable time and does not expect a reply by return of post or an immediate, exclusive "story" (usually involving much research) over the phone.

A great number of addresses of these offices can be obtained from Whitaker. If in doubt as to the offices of some foreign country's publicity bureau, address the inquiry through that country's legation or embassy.

All Governments will, if addressed through their embassies or legations, give any reasonable "public" information about the country. Some Governments run additional services, such, for example, as the Economic Information Service (conducted mainly in English), by the Netherlands Government. From the U.S.A. we have the Bulletin of the Public Affairs Information Service.

For inquiries about local government affairs, apply to individual councillors, if you know any, or to the Town Hall otherwise. Citizens have a right to know what is going on, and very often this information is published. In small communities where the demand for printed reports would not justify the expense, a few typewritten copies are made. One should be in the local central library.

Many enterprising Borough Councils now publish their own news bulletin, news-letter or something similar.

One can 'phone up the public libraries and ask a question, but unless it is the type of question that can be answered almost *ex cathedra*, one should give one's telephone number with the request that one should be rung up when the information is available.

If the librarian cannot answer your question from his own library resources he will usually 'phone up a specialist library.

One could not very well ask a big transport company for details of their running costs. This would be rather impertinent. Yet if one were interested in transport history, the company would probably be pleased to answer inquiries about their early vehicles. They might be willing to give general information as to their future plans. It is all a question of tact. The research worker should ask the question, "If I were in the other fellow's shoes, would *I* give the information? Would the information, if published, create a favourable interest in my business, or would it be scattering hard-learnt experience to the winds—to be used by my business rivals?"

A Letter of Inquiry

If the researcher cannot find the desired information in print, personal inquiry may therefore be made to the right quarter, provided that the question does not presume upon the professional status of the one inquired of, and is not calculated to take up too much time in drafting the reply. To this end, inquiries should be specific, brief, and to the point. Naturally, letters of inquiry should be couched in polite terms so as to give the recipient the impression that the question is to be answered as a favour, and not as a right.

Very often such letters will be unanswered. They may have been ignored or overlooked. Some people find actual writing rather irksome, and put off answering until they finally forget it. Personally I never remind people thus written to that they have forgotten to reply. There are nearly always other people to write to, and it has been my very pleasant experience to find that the majority of people are most polite, helpful and encouraging.

Interviewing

Occasionally it may be necessary to elicit the actual information verbally. Often this is done informally—e.g. a chat with a museum curator. There is a distinct technique in interviewing. First, the time and the place of interview are important. For all professional men and women it is essential to obtain an appointment.

For the purposes of social surveys, etc., where working people, housewives, and so on, have to be interviewed, it is as well to drop on them suddenly and, with a polite introduction, start questioning right away. They are not used to being interviewed, and if a formal appointment was fixed, they would be in a state of some tension. It often happens that one is regarded as a busybody and treated with some suspicion. Answers are given doggedly and discouragingly.

After all, one has only oneself to blame. These people did not ask to be questioned. The interviewer must be rather thick-skinned.

Whilst some people are shy, diffident, or even hostile, others are affable, even garrulous. Sometimes it is as well to let them run on, as they then reveal themselves in their true light, and express their opinion without restraint, making use of their particular idiom and way of speech. At other times it is necessary to elicit some definite information, and if the question is likely to be somewhat daring one, lead up to it gradually. The interviewer should have a carefully prepared list of questions to be asked—to be referred to if either the interviewer or the interviewed becomes tongue-tied, or if the interview deviates from its straight course.

A few notes are necessary, and, indeed, some people are offended if the interviewer does not take down their priceless gems of learning and opinion. On the other hand, some people "dry up" when they see all their words being taken down. They fear they may have committed themselves to certain observations they might afterwards regret. If the interview is to be published, the "copy" should be submitted to the interviewed one, for approval.

Although it is obviously out of the question to travel expensively say, to the Yukon merely to write a short article on the locale of the '49 Gold Rush, one might write a better *book* on the subject if one did so. By the same token, one could possibly write a better book on Famous Q.C.s if one actually interviewed a few. This usually gives an authentic and personal touch to one's work and prevents it from becoming warmed up chunks of other writers' "meat." It is quite true that, in a well written book, the author is almost "speaking" to you personally. But, whenever possible, try to supplement your literary research with personal visits and verbal inquiries.

The fact-finder will obviously find out for himself whether he is better suited to be a digger-up of published information using enough personal inquiries to round off his investigation and give it freshness, or whether he is better suited to be a reporter or interviewer type using enough "background" stuff to fill out. As mentioned in the Preface, those well-known commentators on, say, international affairs, who write so factually (combining "background" material, personal interviews and using, also, exclusive "inside" information) usually employ a team of research workers.

"Suspect" Statistics

Just one other point before we leave the subject of personal inquiries. The research worker will, in certain fields, be presented with various "facts" as established by market-research interviewers, political pollsters, and the like. To save interviewers' time and to make for easier processing of data, the questions to be asked are pre-selected. Though "other comments" are provided for, it is often found that these are treated lightly and not on the same level as the "regular" questions. It could easily happen, therefore, that, without deliberate faking, the "facts" elicited are merely those which support a hoped-for result. To take a comparatively crude example: it was definitely proved that "X" brand of mentholated-licorice-bullseyes was the biggest seller in its field, with sales 23·953 % greater than its nearest competitor. This may be perfectly true. But it may also be a fact (not mentioned in the "poll") that there are only two brands of mentholated-licorice-bullseyes on the market, and their total sales only 0·0007 % of all medicated sweets sold. A questionnaire seeking to establish *all the relevant facts* should take note of such things. You will forgive me, I hope, for bringing in the old aphorism: There are three kinds of lies . . . Lies, Damned Lies and Statistics.

Information from Advertisements

The finances (and therefore, the success) of newspapers and periodicals are bound up with its advertising revenue though to discuss this is far beyond the scope of this present book. What *does* concern us, however, is that advertisements are a source of *information*. The complaint that a particular periodical is "nothing but adverts" is usually counterbalanced by such a remark as "I haven't got down to the article yet. I've been reading the adverts." Current advertisements tell us what is new. It is through these that we often first hear of new materials, tools, foods, equipment for sports and hobbies, and so on. They reflect current taste and trends. The changing cost of commodities compared with wages is all too clearly shown. When we study old advertisements, we find not only pictorial details of dress, articles of furniture, vehicles and the like, with their cost, but are most subtly shown the social customs and conventions of a past age.

A study of advertisements in old issues of periodicals would bring to light some odd facets of social history. (For technical material in advertisements *see* Chapter XI.) A modern advertisement picturing a woman smoking would be illustrating a fact so socially accepted nowadays that it would occasion no adverse comment. But this is a comparatively recent phenomenon. In the early '20's the more daring cigarette advertisements had to make oblique references. One such advertisement shows a girl swimmer, about to dive off a boat. Her male companion is resting at the oars, smoking. She says "Save one for me!" A fascinating study could be compiled on this theme and on other social taboos (and also of tolerances as, for example, of advertisements of cancer "cures") as revealed in older advertisements.

This transition from advertising to social customs, prompts me to mention here that humorous and satirical magazines are happy hunting-grounds for finding details (—especially illustrated ones) of contemporary fads and fancies. Behind many of the old-time jokes concerning, say, drunks, the Squire's lady going "slumming," the adenoidal illiterate maidservant, the village idiot (little concern for the Mentally Handicapped then!) lie object lessons in social history. You think the "Teen-Age Problem" is new? Look up the files of *Punch*, the *Humorist*, *London Opinion*, and the like! (See, for example: Alison Adburgham, **A Punch History of Manners and Modes.**)

Museums

These can be very useful to research workers. In fact, they are intended for such workers.

They are usually specialized, but, if they are mainly general, they often have special collections for which they are noted. We have the Science Museum, the Natural History Museum, the Victoria and Albert (for Art), Geoffrye Museum (old English furniture), the London (London life), etc. Museums collect specimens and exhibits not for the idle gaze of sightseers with nothing better to do, but for the benefit of students who can gain better information about many things by actually seeing them. Some low-budget small-town museum collections are very uninspired and literally warrant the accusation "dry and dusty," but there are others which have admirable collections illustrating bygone local industries, relics of local history, etc.

Museum Catalogues

A museum catalogue, issued at a modest price, and often well illustrated, is a gold mine of authoritative facts. Some are practically textbooks on the subject, and even if one lives hundreds of miles away from the actual exhibits, the photographs and other illustrations make up for this. Secure a catalogue of publications from those museums in which you are interested. Much information can thus be obtained which is not elsewhere published. The British Museum issues several relating to antiquities and the Ancients. The Victoria and Albert Museum has guides to various objects of Art: the Science Museum issues valuable specialized catalogues; many other examples could be quoted.

Co-operating with the Curator

Just as one should make friends with local librarians, so one should make friends with the curator, and never hesitate to ask intelligent questions about the exhibits. Chats with the curators and caretakers will often bring to light strange, interesting, and curious facts, which, properly handled, make acceptable contributions to the popular Press.

Research Work at Museums

All museums have some kind of laboratory and workshop. In the National Museums they are often very extensive, and engage expert chemists, etc. If one has found a strange coin, fossil, bug, etc., which cannot easily be indentified from the usual reference books, it can often be sent to museums for indentification.

It must not be assumed that the museum will act willingly as unpaid valuers, etc., for people who have only a commercial interest in the objects. They hope that they may be sent a rare or unique specimen and be given the chance of acquiring it, by gift or by purchase. They will then have as much interest in the matter as you.

If possible, send the actual specimen along.

Museum Libraries and Inquiries

Many museums, such as the British, Science, and Victoria and Albert, have regular libraries attached. Others have small, semi-private collections of books which interested people can use. Often the curators and directors of various departments can give valuable information concerning the field of knowledge covered by their department.

A book which provides much valuable information is **The Libraries, Museums and Art Galleries Year Book.**

Newspaper Information Bureaux

To create and maintain a faithful circle of readers, most newspapers and magazines encourage readers to write to their various departments for information and advice.

It should not be forgotten that one of the greatest successes in turn-of-the-century popular journalism was *Answers* (to Correspondents). The basic principle still flourishes exceedingly. The current issue of *The Observer* before me contains a "Situations Vacant" advertisement for an "amiably efficient" woman for the "editorial clearing house"—to help deal with readers' inquiries by letter and by 'phone. (The same paper runs a special service of Foreign Affairs news for students and many newspapers run an Intelligence Service.)

Often the readers could have found the information desired in the usual reference books and it is provided from such.

Sometimes the information is of a brief and general nature and if it is about some topic that is brought up dozens of times with every post, such as "Rent Restriction" or "Colic in Budgies," the reply is often in the shape of a "form" letter or a duplicated sheet. On the other hand, some very valuable replies are often received. Not getting very satisfactory advice from one solicitor, the present writer wrote to the legal department of a rather sensational Sunday newspaper. The reply contained absolutely first rate information. Advice on investments, particularly if they do not concern unusually "chancy" ones is often very good.

The information provided is obviously for the *bona-fide* reader who has a problem, and not for professional research workers.

This, however, is a source of information which should not be forgotten. Newspaper librarians are often obliging, and, in any case, are creating goodwill for their paper. They will usually tell you if articles on certain subjects have appeared recently in the columns of their paper.

Trade Papers Information Service

These often have expert advice departments, but the service is confined, as a rule, to regular subscribers, which is only fair, and many such papers are sold by subscription to the "Trade" only.

Other papers may charge a small fixed fee for private information such as valuation and opinion on antiques.

Most of the "practical" and "do-it-yourself" magazines have splendid information services. The only thing they seem to bar is the making of special drawings.

Music

Such musical dictionaries as those of Groves and Collins, and such works as the **Oxford Companion To Music** have already been mentioned. Books on music and musicians can easily be traced from book lists in the manner already described.

Most public libraries have some bound-up sheet music and orchestral scores, though in scope it compares very unfavourably with that of books since, of course, only a small minority of people actually play a musical instrument nowadays. The majority are content to listen, and most public libraries have, nowadays, good collections of gramophone records and reproducing devices for personal and communal listening.

For those requiring music not available in the local library an inquiry to the Central Music Library, housed in the Buckingham Palace Road branch of the Westminster City Libraries may prove fruitful.

The standard catalogue is the **British National Bibliography Music Catalogue.** This started in 1957 and does not include modern "pop" music. The British Museum Reading Room has a splendid collection of music.

A set of gramophone record catalogues forms a useful guide to recorded music. See Darrell, **Encyclopedia of Recorded Music,** and such other works of this nature as **The Gramophone Shop of Recorded Music** (with supplements); **The World's Encyclopedia of Recorded Music,** Clough and Cuming; **Long-Playing Classical Record Catalogue** (The *Gramophone* Magazine).

Though such catalogues *as* catalogues of purchasable records inevitably become obsolete, they continue to give useful information about the chief works of various composers, dates of first performances and so on.

Mention must be made of Barlow and Morgenstern's **Dictionary of Musical Themes** and **Dictionary of Vocal Themes.**

History

Where "Current Affairs" end, and "History" begins is, of course, a moot point. Local History is dealt with on p. 86.

There is no lack of guides to standard books on history. See, for example, the lists given in such compilations as **The Reader's Guide** and **Good Reading** (*see* Chapter V). What follows is just a note or two.

Some excellent "tools" to historical research are—**Bibliography of Historical Writings Published in Great Britain and the Empire.**

International Bibliography of Historical Sciences.

Langer, W. L., **An Encyclopedia of World History.** (Very useful for *dates*.)

A Guide to Historical Literature. This may be kept up to date by referring to the Historical Association's **Annual Bulletin of Historical Literature.**

The publications of the Royal Institute of International Affairs will merit the attention of the serious historian.

Writings on British History. A Bibliography of books and articles on the history of Great Britain from about A.D. 450 to 1914 published during the preceding year (one new volume for each year), with an Appendix containing a select list of writings in that particular year covering British History since 1914.

CHAPTER XIX

ILLUSTRATIONS

ILLUSTRATIONS are often required either (or both) to ascertain visually what cannot adequately be described in print, or to embellish some literary work. Apart from the intrinsic information or story contained in the pictures, illustrations improve the look of the printed page.

Arranging for Illustrations

It is not at all unusual for an author to arrange, personally, for the illustrations (if needed) for his book. Indeed, some publishers' contracts call for this. The author is, at least, expected to be helpful and co-operative, especially where illustrations of unusual subjects are concerned. His editor will usually appreciate being given hints where such illustrations can be obtained. This present book is not, of course, one on journalism, but the writer can affirm, from long experience, that an article sent complete with *appropriate* illustrations stands a far greater chance of acceptance (other things being equal) than one sent without. Anyone who deals with illustrations intended for reproduction should have some idea of the technical processes involved—and the relative costs.

Useful information can be obtained in such books as—

Odham's **Practical Printing and Binding.** This book deals with matters from the Trade point of view.

Illustration and Reproduction. John R. Biggs. This is particularly useful to those who have to deal with fine art illustrations—wood engraving, lithographs, scraper board, pen and wash, etc.

Very useful to all who practise, deal in or are in any way connected with Art is **The Artists' Guide** published by the Artist Publishing Co. (Formerly **The Artists' Year Book.**)

Line and Half-tone

There are two main methods of reproducing illustrations in print—the line block and the half-tone. The first (which is the cheaper, and in many ways the clearer) is used when a drawing or diagram is formed of plain black lines (usually in Indian ink on Bristol board). Intermediate tones are formed by suitable hatching. The "half-tone" block is used for reproducing photographs and wash drawings, such as water-colours. As most of us know, the photographs reproduced in newspapers and magazines are made up of thousands of tiny dots easily visible to the naked eye on the coarser work. The better and more glossy the paper and the finer the "screen," the less noticeable they are.

Water-colours, old coloured prints, etc., must be photographed, and as different colours behave differently on the camera plates, it is a matter of great care to get a really satisfactory reproduction of coloured drawings or objects.

Photostats, Dry Copiers, Micro-films

The photostat is a machine for copying drawings, diagrams, pages of a book, etc. Instead of the usual plate or film, a length of sensitized paper is wound off from the container and used instead. The "negative" consists of white lines on a black ground, and from this, a positive is printed which gives black lines on a white ground, as in the original. By this means pages of rare books may be copied, as well as plates from old out of print Patent Specifications, etc. Many large museums have the apparatus. Where the demand does not warrant the installation, it will often be found that the librarians have arrangements with a local firm (one with a large drawing office, for example) who will get the prints made at cost price, which is quite reasonable. For general reference purposes the negative copy is quite sufficient.

Whilst the photostat has the advantage of taking, if required, negatives larger or smaller than the original "copy," other methods of copying now challenge it, for example, the Xerographic process. Dry-copiers (such, for example, as the *Copycat*) are now much used in the busier libraries. Reference has already been made in this book to the use of these devices for taking copies of selected pages from books in far-distant libraries.

Many of our leading museums have also installed a microfilm apparatus, in which the page of a book is photographed on a tiny film, exquisitely sharp. The whole of a bulky book can be photographed on a small roll of film, and by reversing the process, i.e. viewing the film through a kind of magnifier, the film can be read in the same way as the original page. The saving in space is obvious, and this may solve the growing problem of storing bulky records in libraries. Once the initial cost of the apparatus has been met, the cost of filming is quite low. (*See*, on p. 88, some other remarks regarding microfilms.) *University Microfilms* issue a catalogue of out-of-print books they have re-issued in microfilm or Xerographic form.

Original Drawings

The reader who is gifted with a certain amount of skill in drawing may care to provide his own illustrations. Reference should be made to good books on this subject—as there are certain essential rules to be observed. Drawings should always be at least half as large again as the size they are intended to be reproduced. Lettering, therefore, should be fairly large.

There are professional artists and draughtsmen available to work up one's rough sketches, and if one's research work is being published, the publisher will usually recommend a suitable artist, or arrange for the drawing to be made.

In this connexion I may perhaps be permitted to mention my own book—

Bagley, Wm. A., **Illustrated Journalism** (Hutchinson's Scientific and Technical Publications).

Photograph Agencies

These exist primarily for supplying photographs to the Press, and have not only their own men to cover "diary" events, but a connexion of free-lances who supply them with news pictures and also others of general interest. A list appears in the **Writers' and Artists' Year Book,** from which it can be seen that some specialize in Nature photographs, some in Architecture, some in Portraits, etc. Their files are very extensive, and should the demand be urgent and worth their while, they will take photographs to order.

As a rule they do not like doing business with private people, but prefer to supply established publishers direct.

A fee varying with the size of the reproduction and status of the publication is payable. For book illustration and advertisements, special terms apply. Such Agencies will usually supply prints (for which, of course, a charge is made) for artists' (or others') *reference and study* and not, in this case for reproduction.

The former *Picture Post* photographic library continues as the Radio Times Hulton Picture Library. It must be one of the largest of its kind in existence.

Whilst many of the photographic illustrations used in periodical publications are "Agency" pictures, quite a number are taken by Staff photographers. These pictures are usually available on much the same terms as Agency prints. Editors of picture-papers are frequently asked for copies of certain pictures appearing in the paper, and inquirers are usually put in touch with the supplier. Such journals as *Punch* are frequently asked for permission to reproduce *drawings* that have appeared in the paper.

Nunn, G., **British Sources of Photographs and Pictures** was issued in 1952 and many of the addresses given and figures regarding fees are now quite out of date. One hopes that this book will be re-issued. It is still useful, however, for calling attention to a number of sources.

Publicity Photographs

Publicity photographs are available from a great number of sources, —industrial concerns, marketing boards, design centres, tourist boards, film studios and the like, and often at no cost though, as prints are not cheap to make nowadays, one usually has to have *some* status as a research worker or writer before the prints are forthcoming. In some cases a nominal charge is made for the print(s). Acknowledgment of the source is usually excepted.

For photographs of such things as road accidents due to "drunk driving" it is sometimes possible to get photographs from Police sources.

Copies of lithographed posters, such as those issued by the railway companies and the London Transport Board are much in demand (for inspiration and emulation of technique) by Schools and by Art students. A charge is usually made for these posters.

Art Galleries

Most large towns run an art gallery as well as a library and museum. All are closely allied, and are generally under the care of one committee. All libraries accumulate collections of pictures, usually of local celebrities and old-time engravings of the district. These may be augmented by efforts of the local school of art, as in the writer's own district, and very often the local council purchases works of art, or receives them as gifts. The results of regional photographic surveys may also be housed in the library or art gallery.

In most cases, public libraries possessing collections of mounted photographs, prints and other illustrations lend them, like books, free of charge.

The Library of the Victoria and Albert Museum, London, has a vast collection of photographs on art subjects, and many of the negatives are available for loan. The same can be said of most of our larger national or municipal libraries, and often permission is granted to reproduce the photographs without fee, provided that authority has been obtained, and due acknowledgment made.

A full list of Art Galleries may be seen in the **Libraries, Museums and Art Galleries Year Book.** The readiness with which various galleries allow their exhibits to be reproduced varies. As a rule they prefer to make their own negatives and supply their own prints, although if the picture has to be photographed specially, they do not charge for the negative. Apart from the cost of the print, however, there is the copyright fee to be considered. This is often made even when no copyright exists in the actual picture. The only justification is that the revenue forms an acceptable addition to the Gallery's limited income, whilst, by charging a fee, the picture is not so much likely to be cheapened by over-reproduction.

Many great works of art are suitable for illustrating abstract themes such as "Contentment," "A Lazy Summer Afternoon," etc. Victorian artists loved to paint historical subjects. Other groups preferred Madonnas, Peasant Life, Landscapes, etc.

"Stills" from films are often used as illustrations, especially when dealing with the more seamy side of life.

Small-scale Colour Reproductions

A useful publication is the U.N.E.S.C.O. **Catalogue of Colour Reproductions of Paintings,** consisting of small monochrome reproductions with full information on the best colour reproductions available of each, their size, price and where they are obtainable. In two volumes.

The publishers of modern fine art prints (e.g. Messrs. Frost and Reed) produce, at a reasonable price, a catalogue of prints held. Small reproductions of these are shown, some in colour and some in mono chrome. They are advertised in such magazines as *The Artist*, and are quite useful for studying such artistic matters as choice of subject and viewpoint, composition, colour and tonal scheme, etc. Art Galleries sell coloured post-card size prints of reproductions of famous paintings (as do such publishers as the Medici Society). Here is an excellent way of building up a reference collection of Art Masterpieces, especially as some art books containing many coloured plates are inevitably expensive.

To trace the whereabouts and the value of pictures, see **Art Prices Current** (from 1907).

Art Periodical Indexes

For an author and subject-index to a selected list of fine arts periodicals and museum bulletins (U.S.A., British, and some foreign), see the **Art Index** (U.S.A.), In this we can look up information written by, or about, persons connected with art matters, or contributions concerning technical problems, e.g. airbrush work, or advertisement lay-out.

There is also **The Year's Art,** "a Concise Epitome of all Matters relating to the Arts of Painting, Sculpture, Engraving and Architecture and to Schools of Design": regarded as essential by some librarians despite the time lag in publication resulting in the non-topical nature of some of the information.

Art Books Generally

Although we seem to have branched off into details of Paintings, we must get back to the main theme of illustration (i.e. pictorial facts). During the last decade there has been a great interest in Art generally and in practical, amateur Art in particular . . . a trend which I am glad to notice, continues. Books on Art can be traced through the usual bibliographies.

Slides and Film Strips

Slides or film strips can be borrowed from numerous sources, often free of charge, only the carriage having to be paid. Railways, transport companies, newspapers, and various commercial concerns all have lantern (or projector) slides, usually accompanied by lecture notes.

If an Art Club cannot afford to engage a qualified artist to demonstrate, it can hire a film strip showing a famous artist at work on, say, painting a portrait.

Great strides are being made with educational films, and many interesting facts can be learnt from these. The leading distributors issue catalogues of "interest" and "documentary" films, many of which are issued in sub-standard form for home-projectors.

Portraits in Books

If, for example, we wished to find a portrait of Richard Sheridan we might spend hours looking up first to see who he was and when he lived (a playwright, 1751–1816), and then searching for various biographies or books on English playwrights which might contain his portrait. If we had the **American Library Association (A.L.A.) Portrait Index** (1906) we should be able to look up our subject right away, and find a list of books wherein his portrait appears.

Historical Portraits, 1400–1850, 4 vols. (1909–1919), is a wellproduced collection of full-page portraits of people famous in English History, with biographical desciptions by C. R. L. Fletcher. See also Solly, **Index of Portraits.**

Note that the **Dictionary of National Biography** mentions where portraits may be found (as do some other Biography reference books).

See also the catalogue of the National Portrait Gallery and the **B.M. Catalogue of Engraved British Portraits** (in the Department of Prints and Drawings).

Pictures in Books

One has only to pick up a modern periodical or book, and compare it with older ones, to see what great strides have been made in attractive illustration. Books are lavishly illustrated nowadays, and with a little search we can usually find what we want if our subject is not uncommon. An attempt to form a picture dictionary was the "I See All" Picture Encyclopedia, an alphabetical series of 100,000 pictures of all manner of things and places. Most encyclopedias are well illustrated (foreign ones should not be overlooked), and some announce the fact in their style of title. On occasion, the somewhat quaint illustrations to Le Nouveau Petit Larousse Illustré are useful.

Most children's encyclopedias are profusely illustrated and the adult research worker should not consider it beneath his dignity to seek for illustrations here.

There are, of course, many books composed mainly of pictures, with the minimum of text.

A book which the present writer has found of immense use in looking up illustrations of such common objects as boats, old china, baskets, tools, skeletons, birds, armorial bearings, etc., is Everybody's Enquire Within, edited by Charles Ray. (2 vols., Amalgamated Press: originally issued as a part-work.)

There is the Ellis, J. C., Travel Through Pictures (U.S.A.) (references to pictures in books and periodicals of interesting sites all over the world).

The same authoress has compiled Nature and its Applications. Over 200,000 selected references to nature forms and illustrations of Nature. Also General Index to Illustrations (22,000 selected references in all fields, exclusive of Nature). See also Munro I. and Cook, E. D., Costume Index where we can look up, say, books which will enable us to find pictures of Danish military costumes or eighteenth century skating dress. Cunningham and Beard's Dictionary of English Costume is typical of the modern English books available.

Most public library reference rooms contain useful, well-illustrated books on historical, peasant, etc., costume, furniture styles, peoples of all nations, animals and so on.

Cigarette Cards

Sets of cigarette pictures may provide us with useful data on many subjects. The sale of such sets is now quite a big business, despite the fact that no new cards have been issued for over twenty years.

Some series, e.g. those dealing with Kings and Queens of England, History of Cycling, British Wild Flowers, Stage and Screen Stars of

Yesterday, etc., are, especially if kept in albums that were provided for the purpose, of considerable reference value, and occasionally cover subjects not conveniently dealt with in the usual reference books, nor so well illustrated.

Filing Picture Reference Material

Such a periodical as *Pictorial Education* (the title is self-explanatory) contains useful material. In some public libraries pictorial matter from this magazine and from other sources is often mounted on stiff sheets of paper and is available for reference.

The collection of pictorial references is usually the concern of commercial artists, but the literary research worker may also have the need to file illustrative matter. Where the material consists of photographs, old engravings, and the like, which may eventually be used for book illustration, it may be better to put them in a vertical file, but where the material consists of press cuttings which can be pasted down, reference to a method of classification and filing described in **What the Press Artist Should Know** by John R. Turner (Pitman) will prove fruitful. My own book, **Pictorial Journalism** (Hutchinson), describes a method of filing photographic negatives. I would add that, in cross-indexing photographs, a great deal of labour can be saved by using punched cards (*see* Chapter XVII). Even if we take such a familiar subject as bathing beauties disporting themselves on a beach, we might, later, want to retrieve it in connexion with Holidays, Beach Games, Health and Fitness, Fashions in Swimsuits, Sunnysands (or wherever it was taken), Sunbathing, or in some other category. This more elaborate system of filing refers, of course, to professional or semi-professional activities, and not, usually, to amateur snapshots.

See also—

Howgego, J. L., **Sources of Illustrations.**

Corbett, E. V., **The Illustration Collection** (U.S.A.).

Ireland, N. O., **The Picture File** (U.S.A.).

Many books stress their pictorial content, as for example—

Runes, D. D., **A Pictorial History of Philosophy.**

The Vista **Illustrated Science** series.

The Macdonald **Illustrated Library of Nature** (Science, etc.).

CHAPTER XX

YOUR PERSONAL LIBRARY

IT is obvious that the research worker has to do much of his work in large libraries. Nevertheless, he should own a considerable private library.

Much time is spent in travelling to and from libraries and waiting for books, so that a writer who has the books at hand enjoys an obvious advantage.

It is impossible to give a list of recommended books for the home reference library—tastes differ so much. There are, too, so many editions of standard books, such as dictionaries, and the like, varying in price, etc., that one cannot be dogmatic. (I exclude, in this chapter, purely "recreational" reading.)

There are many series of books such as the well-known *Everyman Library*, "*Teach Yourself . . .*", the *Penguins* and *Pelicans* etc., specially catering for the home library. It is well worth while getting a catalogue (usually annotated) of books in such series.

Perhaps the best advice is: read this book carefully. Then visit library reference rooms, looking up as many of the mentioned books as you can; get to know such books as Chambers's **Book of Days.** Some volumes will not appeal: others you will wish to own. These last may be purchased. Others may be obtained from second-hand booksellers. If, as you should, you specialize, build up a collection of books, old and new (with indexed files of one or two periodicals) dealing with your hobbyhorse. See McColvin, Lionel, **The Personal Library**; Haines, Helen E., **Living With Books,** "a guide to the evaluation and use of the hundreds of sources of information on books."

Do You Need an Encyclopedia?

With *Whitaker* and *Pears* alone, a great deal can be done. Whether to acquire an encyclopedia or not is a moot point. There are those who say that since a large (and expensive) encyclopedia is readily available at the nearest public library, the money that might have been spent by a private individual on obtaining an encyclopedia might better be spread over buying separate standard and reference books. *Contra:* others (myself included) say that it seriously interrupts concentration on one's work if what is normally only five minutes' reference in an encyclopedia readily to hand develops into

a half-day at the local library (and *if* there is a library conveniently
"round the corner"). Personally I would opt for the best encyclopedia I could afford, taking into consideration whether one had
much reference work, professional, semi-professional or casually
amateur to do and also, in some cases, whether it would be of
assistance to other members of the family.

The production of a new major encyclopedia is an extremely
costly matter. It may be possible to cut costs, say, by producing the
work internationally so that all the illustrations can be used
again. But I have known cases where a new cheap encyclopedia is
just an old one (taken over by a new publisher) and brought seem-
ingly up to date by hack writers.

Second-hand Booksellers

A brief note here on second-hand booksellers (or "antiquarian
booksellers" as they prefer to style themselves nowadays). These
should not be confused with second-hand dealers who may have a
row of books (mostly out-of-date and unreadable novels) for sale.
Nor should we be misled by the shabby façade of low-priced books
which line the outside of the dealer's front window and half-obstruct
his doorway. He thinks so little of these castaways that he rarely
protects them from the weather. His main business—involving
considerable bibliographical knowledge—is to buy up *good*
libraries (possibly of deceased scholars) to classify the books, noting
rarities, and, through a catalogue (the best are properly printed), to
offer them anew to book users. He performs an invaluable service
in making out-of-print books available. If the book you require
is not in his stock, he will "search" for it (i.e. advertise for it in his
trade paper).

Most antiquarian booksellers will send you their catalogues . . .
usually free, although a nominal charge is sometimes made. The
better class catalogues are usually annotated, especially for the
better-paying items and one can pick up useful bibliographical
knowledge from them (*see* Chapter V). If you prove to be a fairly
steady purchaser, the booksellers will, naturally, put you on their
regular mailing lists.

But do not imagine that you are going to get the books at "six-
penny box" or "jumble sale" prices!

Paperbacks

And here seems a good place to mention paperback books.
Although there is a growing use of these (suitably re-bound) in

public libraries, they are still mainly purchased by book-lovers for home use.

Most readers except, perhaps, the very youngest, will doubtless be familiar with the so-called "Paperback Revolution" in book publishing. Cheap fiction in paper covers has been with us for a long time, but it was left to Penguin Books in the mid '30's to put quality and "class" into paperbacks and, a little later, with their Pelican series, to bring out cultural books in a similarly inexpensive form. For a time, Penguin Books were by far the leading publishers of paperbacks, but naturally, their success encouraged competitors, some of whom began to bring paperbacks into disrepute with trashy fiction bearing gaudy and in some cases, "suggestive," pictorial covers.

Whilst many still regard paperbacks as comparatively cheap books to read say, on a train journey or on the beach at holiday times, developments have occurred which make the generally accepted term *paperback* somewhat misleading. Most of the leading publishers of "hardbacks" have entered the field. They have selected from their back-lists certain worth-while books—often quite scholarly or quite technical—and have re-issued them as paperbacks. (Some books, of course, are specially written for, or have their first publication as paperbacks.) Except, then, that they have "soft" covers, these latter paperbacks (which can cost up to thirty shillings each, though the majority are more "popularly" priced) have little in common with the ephemeral publications previously alluded to.

A point worth remembering is that though a paperback edition may be—as a paperback—newly published, it may be a re-issue, in this form, of a standard "hardback" book, possibly one that has been out of print and might not have been re-issued at all were it not for the economics of paperback publishing.

The sectionalized lists in a catalogue of paperbacks can act, to some extent, as bibliographies.

Whitaker's Reference Catalogue of **Paperbacks (in print and on sale in Great Britain)** is published twice-yearly. It is classified by subject, with author and title indexes. It also includes such additional information as a list of paperback publishers and their addresses, with the names of the series published by each.

A less detailed catalogue (17 sections as against Whitaker's 55) is **Paperbacks in Print** published quarterly by Hansom Books Ltd. New titles in this book are underlined. For the American side see **Paperbound Books in Print** (R. R. Bowker Co., New York), revised quarterly.

Many standard reference works can now be obtained as paperbacks.

Writing Up

It is beyond the scope of the present book to go into details of the actual writing up of the information gained by one's research. In addition to having a good dictionary, the writer will usually have, within convenient reach, such standard works as Fowler's **Modern English Usage** (though as this work was originally written in 1926, some of the recommendations are no longer strictly current despite corrections in later editions). Two books by the late G. H. Vallins (**Good English** and **Better English**) are highly spoken of, whilst Sir Ernest Gowers' **Plain English,** written originally as a guide for Civil Servants, exerts a beneficial influence on us all even if (as with other guides) we do not regard *every* recommendation as sacrosanct.

Eric Partridge's **Usage and Abusage** was designed not to compete with Fowler but to supplement it and to complement it, especially for the period from 1926.

Another work which brings Fowler up to date is Margaret Nicholson's **A Dictionary of American-English Usage.** There is also **A Dictionary of Modern American Usage** by H. W. Horwill.

The Technical Writer (Godfrey and Parr) is excellent in its field and has a useful bibliography appended. See also **Technical Publications** (C. Baker); **Industrial Editing** (B. Smith); **A Guide to Technical Writing** (J. Baker); **Writing A Technical Paper** (D. H. Menzel).

CHAPTER XXI

A FINAL CHECK

THIS is hardly the kind of book that one reads straight through and then says "Well, that's *that*." It is a book to be referred to again and again and its recommendations put into practice in so far as they concern one's special requirements in the way of fact-finding.

Know Your Reference Books

Once again I would ask you to examine personally, and thoroughly, the leading reference books I have named. Do you know exactly what you can expect to find in, say, **Whitaker's Almanack** or **Pears Cyclopedia**? Would you be able to, say, write about "Marks on Italian porcelain"? Something about that in **Pears,** surely? Have you ever *looked* inside, say, the **20th Century D.N.B.** or **Who Was Who** or are these still mere names in my book? Have you ever made the effort to find a copy of, and look up some references in, say, **Poole's Index** or (if a Londoner) sought information from, say, a Manchester telephone directory?

Were I commissioned by a Transatlantic publisher to write this book I should probably be asked to make the title: "It's Fun To Find Out." There are few of us who have not been caught in the lure of an encyclopedia. We intend to look up, say, Taoism, but the eye is caught by Tally Office and after reading this, we flip over a page or two too many and find ourselves reading about Tapioca or Tapirs.

This is a tendency which must be strictly checked when we are concentrating on a specific inquiry, but it does show that an encyclopedia can be a fascinating work. And so can other reference works. For very special inquiries we may have to trace rather obscure sources: sources used, perhaps, once in a lifetime. But for "background" knowledge it is far better to know, inside out, the content of, say, twenty leading reference books than to have mere catalogue acquaintance with two hundred or two thousand.

But even after the first reading of this book you will be in a better position to answer the questions propounded in the General Line of Inquiry (Chapter III), and after every reading and study of component parts, be able to take the questions on a higher level, so to speak. You will, I hope, be able to seek information on these subjects not specifically dealt with in this book. The Preface explained why it was not possible or even desirable to try to give a "dictionary"-form list of sources.

The Arrangement of this Book

It may be relevant, at this point, to explain the arrangement of this book. The information might have been given in the Preface but it involved a discussion of cataloguing systems which could be appreciated only after reading about these things later on in the body of this book.

The subjects might have been arranged by Decimal Classification and such things as Travel and Geography (91) and History (91) brought together with Biography (92) closely following. Such an arrangement is followed in the extensive **Guide to Reference Material** (soon to be described). In this present book (which makes no claims to complete coverage) I have grouped the material more for matters of convenience. For example, as explained in Chapter VII, the border line between an encyclopedia and a dictionary is somewhat difficult to define. So although there are, to the classification expert, distinct differences, I have, for the novice fact-finder, grouped Encyclopedias and Dictionaries together. And so with other subjects. In this I have precedent in the practice of many reference librarians who shelve, ready to hand near the Inquiry counter, a number of the most-used reference books, taken out of the main classification sequences. And Winchell in her **Guide to Reference Books** (*see* notes to come) uses her own classification and not the U.D.C.

In deciding what subjects to cover, I followed for simplicity the main classifications of the New Books catalogue-bulletin issued by my local library. These are—(the remarks in brackets refer to my own book) Bibliography (treated extensively), Philosophy and Religion (passing notes and references to a large anthology only), Social Sciences (confined to a note or two on a famous bibliography and an encyclopedia, together with references to Government publications), Languages (treated under Dictionaries), Science (a complete new chapter written for this edition), Technology (treated under Science and also reference to certain directories), Fine Arts (chiefly as Illustrations), Music (some notes), Games, Sports and Entertainments (references to typical Year Books), Literature (extensively treated), Travel and Geography (Topography and discussion of maps, etc., and travel guides), Biography (extensively treated), History (some notes), Fiction (treated under Bibliography, Literature and Books in Print, etc.). There is, as you will have found, much else, dealing with the use of books, etc., as this present book is not just a series of annotated book lists.

There are two extremely useful reference books (already briefly alluded to) which will help you round off your inquiries into any other subject coming within the usual classifications used in general reference work. I allude to such things as Law, Economics, Religion, Transport, and so on.

Guides to Reference Books and Material

Though chiefly compiled for professional librarians as guidance in the building up of reference library "stock" the (British) Library Association's **Guide to Reference Material** is extremely useful, also, to the individual research worker.

It provides an annotated list of the leading current reference books and bibliographies to various subjects, with an accent on those published in Great Britain. Technology is given special prominence. Though at first it appears to rival the U.S.A. work cited below, it actually supplements it.

The transatlantic counterpart of the above book is the American Library Association's **Guide to Reference Books.** It is international in scope, though coverage is unevenly spread and Science is not quite so well treated as in the English book. For U.S.A. sources it is unrivalled. It is based on earlier works and the edition before me (Ed: Constance M. Winchell) contains an essay on "Reference Work and Reference Books" which is well worth reading. The annotations are also worth studying.

Both of these reference books are kept up to date with Supplements. They can usually be consulted in the Reference Room of a public library.

The **ASLIB Directory** has been described elsewhere.

As hinted in the Preface, this book tells you how to make the best of the library services and the fully-trained, professional librarian's expertise. If you look at some of the more advanced books for professional librarians, especially those dealing with science libraries, you will realize how much "know-how" is needed to collect, index, store and retrieve published facts.

Some Further Reading

There are some more general books on reference library work and administration which the research worker can read with profit. Typical examples are—

Introduction to Reference Books. Roberts, A. D.

Reference Library Stock. McColvin, L. R., and Collison, R. L. W.

See, too, the Publications List of the Library Association.

Ask Yourself Questions

It is a good mental excercise to set oneself posers, and think of how the desired information could be obtained. For example these are some questions I set myself to pass the time away whilst waiting for a train.

Where could I find out—

Who was President of Mexico in 1896?
What kind of surgical instruments did the Ancient Romans use?
What was the first newspaper published in Norwich?
How many dentists practise in Johannesburg?
How many books has Sir Winston Churchill published?
What is the Eskimo word for long woollen "pants"?
Name some of the (a) earliest, (b) latest books on Malaria.
Where was Mr. Arnold Bennett living in 1930?
Is there any Purchase Tax in Sweden?
Where could I get an illustration of old St. Paul's Cathedral?
Do any unpublished posthumous works of Johann Strauss II exist, and if so, where?
How did English toys sell in Belgium last year?
Who is currently the chief legal luminary in the State of Wyoming?
Is there a Trade directory of fish-fryers?

To a layman, these questions are terribly "stiff." To an expert researcher, they are quite easy. Where, reader, would YOU look? There is no need actually to get the final details. The whole point is, in which direction would you go?

Some years ago there was quite a craze for propounding such questions, and most newspapers carried a "General Knowledge" feature every day. Several books of this type appeared. The craze has now somewhat abated, but certain journals still, on occasion, carry such features, "popular," difficult or literary, according to the tone of the paper. We are asked, for example, "What author was the son of a doorkeeper in the House of Commons?" It is only by sheer chance that the reader could answer this at once from his own knowledge. But he could find out.

Analysing Sources of Information

After reading a book, or article in a periodical, which is packed with facts, it is useful to speculate how the author obtained his information; how much was culled from published sources; how much from special inquiries, and so on. In order to give authenticity to their books, many authors list special sources of information, as—to take a random example—Peter Fleming in the preface to his *Invasion 1940*. He mentions such sources as the Historical Section of the

Cabinet Office and of the Air Ministry; *The Times* Intelligence
Department, the staff of the Imperial War Museum and the Writers'
and Speakers' Research. He admits difficulty in getting information
from official archives.

Hesketh Pearson, the biographer of Gilbert and Sullivan, Oscar
Wilde, Sydney Smith, and others, gives long lists of "Authorities."
That on *Gilbert & Sullivan* contains about a hundred entries. It is
rather unlikely that the author collected all the books named before
he sat down to write. It seems more probable that one book led to
another: one may have mentioned (for example) the *Gilbert &
Sullivan Journal*, and this journal mentioned other books. The
author cites some unpublished correspondence, and acknowledges
some personal help received.

When analysing certain "feature" articles, bear in mind that some
of the information may be specially purchased. Newspaper offices
are always being approached by people who have a "story to sell"—
sometimes in dubious circumstances. Most people who serve the
"famous" (personal servants, confidential secretaries, private
detectives and the like), usually have a clause in their contract which
forbids them, for a certain period after leaving the job to disclose
personal details of their former employers. Many are tempted to
break the terms of their contract, such is the lure of the lucre offered
by sensational journals of minimal morals.

Of course much "inside information" is quite legitimately dis-
closed after various formalities have been observed. Some people
resign their positions before writing. There are "perks" in most
professions, and many leading politicians, war-time generals, retired
C.I.D. men, and the like, find it profitable to pen their "now it can
be told" stuff. The critical research worker may well examine this
type of thing very minutely. There is no doubt that much of the
appeal comes from having the story told personally by those who
were engaged in the events at first hand. And there are some who
have a unique "first person" story to tell. But as regards actual *facts*,
much of the information was available already to diligent research
workers.

Reviewers who are also writers are often concerned with the
"mechanics," so to speak, of a book. Research workers can take
note of such things as the following—

In a *Daily Telegraph* review of **English Historical Documents**,
Vol. XI (1783–1832) Robert Birley (Headmaster of Eton College
and a teaching historian), writes—

   . . . this is no ordinary historical anthology. There are nearly 600
   pieces. Of these about 90 come from reports of Parliamentary debates

and the papers of Parliamentary Committees; about 200 are from books, at least half of them from works which the interested man in the street would be very unlikely to have met; no fewer then 221 come from unpublished manuscripts. This last category is the most remarkable feature of the book.

John Gunther, author of the famous "Inside" books (*Inside Europe . . . Africa . . . U.S.A. . . . Latin America*, etc.), which are packed tight with information has (1962) written a small volume: **The Story of the Inside Books (a "Fragment of Autobiography").**

Though intended for the general reader, the author gives, especially in his last chapter, some useful technical hints regarding press-cuttings, note-writing, the technique of interviewing and some notes on his methods of writing and revising. Earlier in the book we have interesting details of how the fact-finding trips were organized and financed.

Signing Off . . .

In any book of this kind, the great difficulty is always to know where to leave off. There is just *one* more reference work that insists on being mentioned. And, on reflection, if *that* goes in, surely we must mention *such and such*, otherwise perceptive readers will think the author negligent in overlooking it. In trying vainly to achieve completeness one risks wearying the general reader who, by this time, is probably saying, in effect, "Please leave me something to find out for myself."

Exactly! Over to you . . . . . over!

NOTE ON USING THE INDEX

THIS work has been planned in such clear-cut divisions and with so few cross-references that a study of the Table of Contents (page x) is recommended. Attention is also drawn to the Preface, wherein it is explained that most of the books cited in this present volume are given as *examples only*.

Whilst, for example, Fodor's Travel Guide is mentioned (page 85), it is but typical of a host of others. It is impossible to mention them all, nor is it necessary. Yet it would be invidious in this Index to call attention to one book (mentioned only in passing) when others, equally good, cannot be listed. For remarks on travel guides, therefore, look in this Index, under Guide Books, or Tourist Information or Travel Guides.

On the other hand, there are a number of standard reference books (e.g. *Whitaker's Almanack* or the *Dictionary of National Bibliography*) which have been more specially annotated in the text. Entries for these, under their own names, appear in this Index.

INDEX

145